SpringerBriefs in Energy

For further volumes:
http://www.springer.com/series/8903

Enrique Querol · Borja Gonzalez-Regueral
Jose Luis Perez-Benedito

Practical Approach to Exergy and Thermoeconomic Analyses of Industrial Processes

Springer

Enrique Querol
School of Mining Engineering
Technical University of Madrid (UPM)
Madrid
Spain

Borja Gonzalez-Regueral
School of Mining Engineering
Technical University of Madrid (UPM)
Madrid
Spain

Jose Luis Perez-Benedito
Aeronautical and Aerospace
Engineering School
Technical University of Madrid (UPM)
Madrid
Spain

Additional material to this book can be downloaded from http://extras.springer.com/

ISSN 2191-5520 ISSN 2191-5539 (electronic)
ISBN 978-1-4471-4621-6 ISBN 978-1-4471-4622-3 (eBook)
DOI 10.1007/978-1-4471-4622-3
Springer London Heidelberg New York Dordrecht

Library of Congress Control Number: 2012948183

Printed on acid-free paper

Springer is part of Springer Science+Business Media (www.springer.com)

Preface

The aim of this book is to enable the reader to perform the necessary calculations for an exergetic analysis (thermodynamics) and a thermoeconomic analysis (process costs) of any industrial process.

Using the presented methodology, a deeper understanding and analysis of an example process will be obtained throughout the book. This process is an innovative working cycle that uses the exhaust gases from the gas turbine coupled with the compressor of a natural gas compression station. This kind of station is used in natural gas pipelines to recover the pressure needed by the gas to flow.

The chosen cycle is an ammonia–water cycle. Throughout this book, all the concepts and calculations needed are broken down using the thermodynamic data obtained from an Aspen Plus® simulation. The use of a simulation is greatly beneficial because it makes available the thermodynamic data needed for the calculation of the exergy of the process streams.

Hand-made calculations for obtaining thermodynamic data are also explained, although the procedure can be difficult, since the following data are needed for each matter stream:

- composition
- mass flow
- pressure
- temperature
- enthalpy increment between two states
- entropy increment between two states
- chemical exergy of the substances, or their free energy of formation
- kinetic and potential energy if their variation is important in the process

Also, the work values are needed, as well as the heat flows' value and the temperature at which they are produced.

All the calculations of the example used are done in a spreadsheet. Matrix algebra is continuously used to release calculations from the size and complexity of any facility. Valuable and additional material is available on a web page hosted by Springer http://www.springer.com/978-1-4471-4621-6. This material is referenced in the text to avoid including an excessive number of tables and numbers in the text.

When there is a clear added value for a better understanding of the analysis done and/or the process improvement possibilities, results are displayed in two ways; numerically (in tables) and graphically.

The authors would like to express their shared thanks to Prof. Jose M. Montes for all his efforts and dedication, as well as the valuable contributions he has made throughout the preparation of this book. The authors would also like to express their shared thanks to the Polytechnical University of Madrid and especially the School of Mines from which the three of them graduated as Mining engineers and where this book has been conceived and written.

The authors wish to express their gratitude to their families and friends for their support, as well as the unselfish work of those who have contributed to the fulfillment of this book.

Madrid, Spain The Authors

The following information is available in the website:

Documents

`Doc1001`: Aspen Plus® flowsheet of the example process used in the book (Figs. 1.2 and 1.3).
`Asp1002`: Aspen Plus® v.7 simulation files of the book example process.
`Doc1003`: RPI classification of the example process.
`Doc1099`: list of errors.
`Doc2001`: Aspen Plus® flowsheet of a combined cycle.
`Asp2002`: Aspen Plus® v.7 simulation files of a combined cycle.
`Doc2002`: Brief description of the combined cycle.
`Doc2003`: RPI classification of the combined cycle.

Workbooks

`WB1001`: Workbook with the data obtained from the simulator in three sheets: `m` for matter streams, `W` for Work streams, and `Q` for Heat streams.
`WB1011`: Workbook with the calculations done for the case studied in the book.

The structure of the book is as follows:

Sheet	Name	Content
1	`m`	Data obtained from the simulator (Matter streams)
2	`W`	Data obtained from the simulator (Work streams)
3	`Q`	Data obtained from the simulator (Heat streams)
4	`BCorrM`	Data selected from the matter streams simulator data (BCorrM) and calculation of the physical and chemical exergy of the matter streams
5	`MHBT`	Selected data for the matter streams as well as the Matter, Energy and Exergy vectors. Also vectors, calculations and results are present for: Exergy Cost, Unit exergetic cost, Thermoeconomic cost, unit exergoeconomical cost.
6	`A`	Incidence and costs matrixes
7	`Eq`	Results for the pieces of equipment
8	`R`	Resource Matrix
9	`P`	Products Matrix
10	`I`	Losses Matrix
11	`Report`	Report with a summary of all the results obtained

`WB2001`: Example 2 workbook with the data obtained from the simulator in three sheets: `m` for matter streams, `W` for work streams, and `Q` for heat streams.
`WB2004`: Example 2 workbook with the fixed cost data (Z) of each equipment unit.

> The text inside a grey textbox like this refers to additional information available in the book website in Springer.

Contents

Acronyms

AER	Stable reference environment in the MHBT
CCS	Cascade condensation system
EAC	Equipment acquisition cost
EXXX	Heat exchanger being XXX numbers
FC	Fixed costs
HHV	High heating value
HP	High pressure
HRSG	Heat recovery steam generator
IEC	Installed equipment cost
LHV	Low heating value
LP	Low pressure
MHBT	Mass, heat, exergy and thermoeconomics
OM	Operation and maintenance
PEC	Total purchasing cost of the equipment
PXXX	Pumps, being XXX numbers
R/P/I	Resource, product and inert
SRE	Stable reference environment
SXXX	Separator, being XXX numbers
TCI	Total capital investment
TXXX	Turbine, being XXX numbers
WBXX	Workbook, indicating the version by the four numbers after WB
ZXXX	Stream used for calculating its exergy in Aspen Plus®, being XXX numbers

Symbols

Symbol	Description	Units
b_{int}	Mass specific internal exergy	[kJ kg^{-1}]
b_{ch}	Mass specific chemical exergy	[kJ kg^{-1}]
$\tilde{b}_{ch,i}$	Molar specific chemical exergy	[kJ kmol^{-1}]
b_{phys}	Mass specific physical exergy	[kJ kg^{-1}]
B	Exergy	[kJ]
$\dot{B}$	Exergy flow	[kW]
B^*	Flow exergetic cost vector	[kW]
$\Phi_{(n\times1)}$	Assigned thermoeconomic cost vector	[€ s^{-1}]
c_p	Mass specific heat at constant pressure	[kJ kg^{-1} K^{-1}]
$\tilde{c}_v$	Molar specific heat at constant volume	[kJ kmol^{-1} K^{-1}]
$\tilde{c}_p$	Molar specific heat at constant pressure	[kJ kmol^{-1} K^{-1}]
$\tilde{g}_{fo,i}$	Molar standard free energy	[kJ kmol^{-1}]
h	Mass specific enthalpy	[kJ kg^{-1}]
$\tilde{h}$	Molar specific enthalpy	[kJ kmol^{-1}]
Δh_{vap}	Vaporization enthalpy	[kJ kg^{-1}]
$H_{(n\times1)}$	Energy vector	[kW]
$\dot{H}$	Enthalpy	[kW]
HHV	High Heating Value	[kJ kmol^{-1}]
LHV	Low Heating Value	[kJ kmol^{-1}]
$\dot{m}$	Mass flow	[kg s^{-1}]
M	Molecular mass	[kg kmol^{-1}]
$\dot{n}$	Molar flow	[kmol s^{-1}]
p	Pressure	[Pa]
Q	Heat	[kJ]
$\dot{Q}$	Heat flow	[kW]
R	Gas constant (mass base)	[kJ kg^{-1} K^{-1}]
$\tilde{R}$	Gas constant (molar base)	[kJ kmol^{-1} K^{-1}]

(continued)

(continued)

Symbol	Description	Units
s	Mass specific Entropy	[kJ kg^{-1} K^{-1}]
$\tilde{s}$	Molar specific Entropy	[kJ $kmol^{-1}$ K^{-1}]
T	Temperature	[K]
$\tilde{u}$	Specific internal energy (molar base)	[kJ $kmol^{-1}$]
W	Work	[kJ]
$\dot{W}$	Work flow	[kW]
x	Molar fraction	[°/1]
σ	Stefan-Boltzmann coefficient	[W m^{-2}]
η	Efficiency	[%] or [°/1]
v	Specific volume	[m^3 kg^{-1}]
Ω	Assigned exergetic cost vector	[kW]

Chapter 1
Introduction

Abstract The purpose of this chapter is twofold. On the one hand, to introduce the principal characteristics of thermoeconomics, a discipline that will be used throughout the book. On the other hand, to present an example system for the application of the concepts developed in a practical way. Once the physical process has been described, indicating the main pieces of equipment and its streams, a flow diagram for its simulation is shown and described using Aspen Plus®, as well as the main criteria adopted for the simulation. Lastly, a subdivision of the system is proposed, in order to ease its study, in two different subsystems (although a complete and detailed study, with the lowest aggregation level, is shown and can be followed on the website of this book).

1.1 Introduction

Thermoeconomics is the branch of power engineering that, by means of the combined application of thermodynamics and economics, allows the attainment of results otherwise impossible through traditional thermodynamic and economic analysis [4]. The fundamental difference lies in the use of the Second Law of Thermodynamics and the concept of exergy. Exergy is taken as a rational basis for economic cost allocation between the resources and products involved in industrial processes and for the economic evaluation of their thermodynamic imperfections. All this constitutes a substantial contribution to the analysis, evaluation and optimization of industrial systems.

When a single product is obtained through a given system, its production cost will simply be the sum of all incurred costs, which is calculated through a cost balance. In the case of multiple products, as many equations as products are required to distribute the costs among the products obtained. Exergy provides a thorough criterion for the formulation of these equations and the subsequent determination of individual production costs. For example, in the case of any cogeneration system, two products are usually available, heat and power. In these cases it would make no sense to determine the costs of heat and power output proportionally to their

E. Querol et al., *Practical Approach to Exergy and Thermoeconomic Analyses of Industrial Processes*, SpringerBriefs in Energy,
DOI: 10.1007/978-1-4471-4622-3_1, © The Author(s) 2013

energies. The appropriate course of action is to allocate the costs proportionally to their exergies, which adequately reflects their respective useful effects. If costs were simply allocated proportionally to the energy content of the products, then an excessive cost would be given to heat and an insufficient cost to power.

In general terms the purposes of thermoeconomics are the following:

- To calculate the costs of all the streams in the process analyzed.
- To analyze the cost formation process and flow inside industrial processes.
- To evaluate the costs of exergy destruction and losses.
- To aid the user in the task of optimizing the performance of each component of a system and of the system as a whole.
- To aid the user in the task of optimizing the cost of the system's products.

Thermoeconomic analysis is quite a versatile tool, as it can be used for a whole industrial process, only part of it or even a piece of equipment of the process, in each case making use of the aggregation level needed by the engineer for a better understanding and improvement of the process. It can also be used in all engineering fields. Nowadays it is mainly used to quantify and study energy optimizations, with the aim of reducing the resources consumed, or increasing the products obtained with a given resource consumption, but it has also been suggested as an appropriate tool for environmental and energy policies.

For example, comparing the exergy destruction costs in a piece of equipment with its investment costs can be used to determine whether the exergy saving provided by some improvement in its efficiency justifies the larger investment it will probably require. These calculations are extremely useful when making decisions for improvement. When it comes to a complex system, the use of successive approximations, guided by thermoeconomics constitutes what is probably the best practical optimization resource today.

1.2 Example System

Along the different chapters of this book, as an application example, a complete exergetic and thermoeconomic analysis is conducted on an electricity generation system. This system is a $NH_3 + H_2O$ cycle coupled to the turbine exhaust gases of a compression station for a natural gas network. The basic outline of the compressor station can be seen in Fig. 1.1.

The compression station houses a gas turbine using natural gas in order to move the centrifugal compressor of the main gas line. The outgoing exhaust gases from the expansion body are directed towards a flue for disposal to the environment.

In Fig. 1.1, one possible alternative for the improvement of the energy usage in this kind of facility is shown. The system proposed for electricity generation comprises a closed $NH_3 + H_2O$ cycle, which uses the exhaust fumes of the gas turbine as a heat source, and the environment the as cold sink. The installed capacity of this cycle is of 3.6 MW. Figures 1.2 and 1.3 show the diagram of the generation system under analysis.

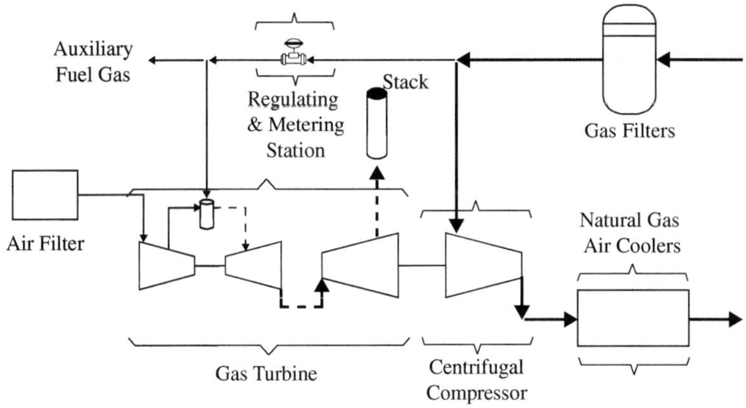

Fig. 1.1 Simplified diagram of a compression station, featuring the turbine compressor

The heat recovery steam generator consists of an economizer, an evaporator and a superheater (E916, E915 and E914) to produce a high temperature gaseous stream (94107) using the gas turbine exhaust gases 90103 from the compressor station's turbine. The superheated steam from the boiler (stream 94107) expands in the turbine T971 to 4 bar. This pressure is 4 times higher than the atmospheric pressure due to three main reasons:

- Allows the use of cheaper and more compact cycles (especially important for turbine and condenser sizes and costs).
- Ensures that under no circumstances air enters the working fluid circuit.
- Ensures that the condensation can be done with a fluid (water or air) at environmental temperature.

Owing to the azeotropic character of the mixture used, more equipment is needed to condense the working fluid, which makes use of regenerators (to reduce the old working fluid temperature, increasing the temperature of the new working fluid), two condensers (to condense two different vapour streams of different NH_3/H_2O ratio) and two pumps. As the lighter component of the mixture needs a lower temperature to condense, the working fluid 94109 is mixed with stream 96102 to increase the water content and reduce the condensation temperature of the resulting stream 97101. To increase again the NH_3 content, a flash (S921) is then used to obtained the richest NH_3 stream of the process (95102) which is mixed with 97109 in the quantity needed to obtained the desired NH_3 content of the working fluid (stream 94102).

After the steam turbine T971 the high enthalpy of stream 94108 will be used to heat the fluid (stream 97106) which goes to the separator S921 through the regenerator E921. This mixture is outgoing from the turbine T971, and cooled in Regenerator I E921 is mixed with a fluid depleted in ammonia (stream 96101) generated by the separator S921.

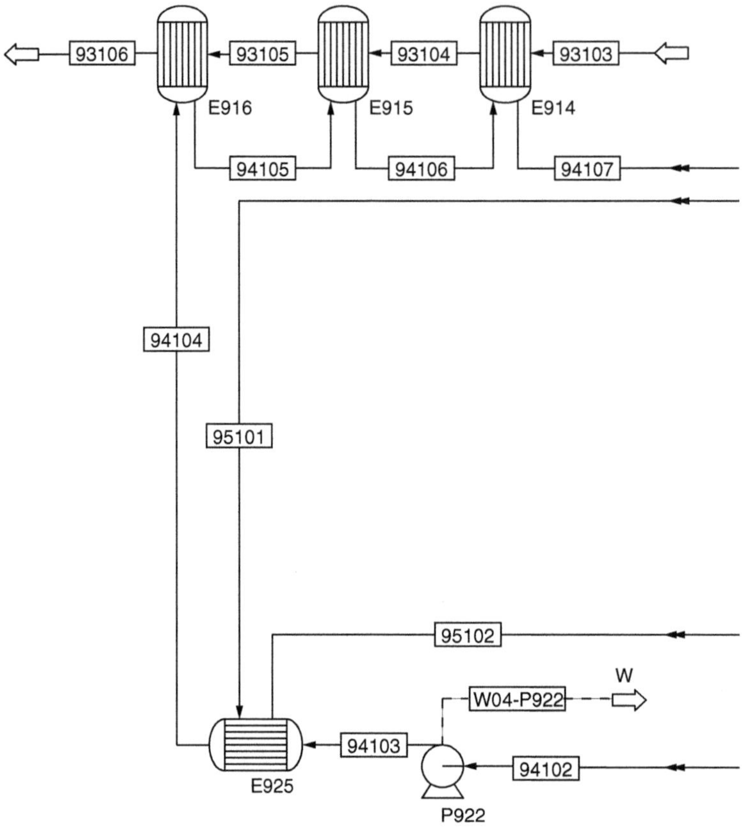

Fig. 1.2 Aspen Plus® flowsheet (1 of 2)

This process is necessary to dilute the NH_3 present in the fluid that enters in a second regenerator (E923) and in the low pressure condenser (E922), so that the condensation temperature rises to enable the use of an ambient fluid (water from a river is assumed in the example process to be the ambient fluid, although a condensing tower, or an aerocondenser can also be used).

The condensate (stream 97103) then is pumped (P921) to 9 bar (stream 97104), and divided into two branches, one (stream 97105) that feeds the separator S921, and another (stream 97109) which goes to the high pressure condenser E924 after being mixed with an ammonia rich gas stream 95102.

The fluid from the reflux branch (stream 97105) is heated in two steps in the Regenerators I (E923) and II (E922) streams 97106 and 97108, before entering the separator, so that after passing through the pump, it reaches the temperature and pressure conditions for the separator to generate liquid and gaseous flows, whose composition is tailored to the needs of the cycle.

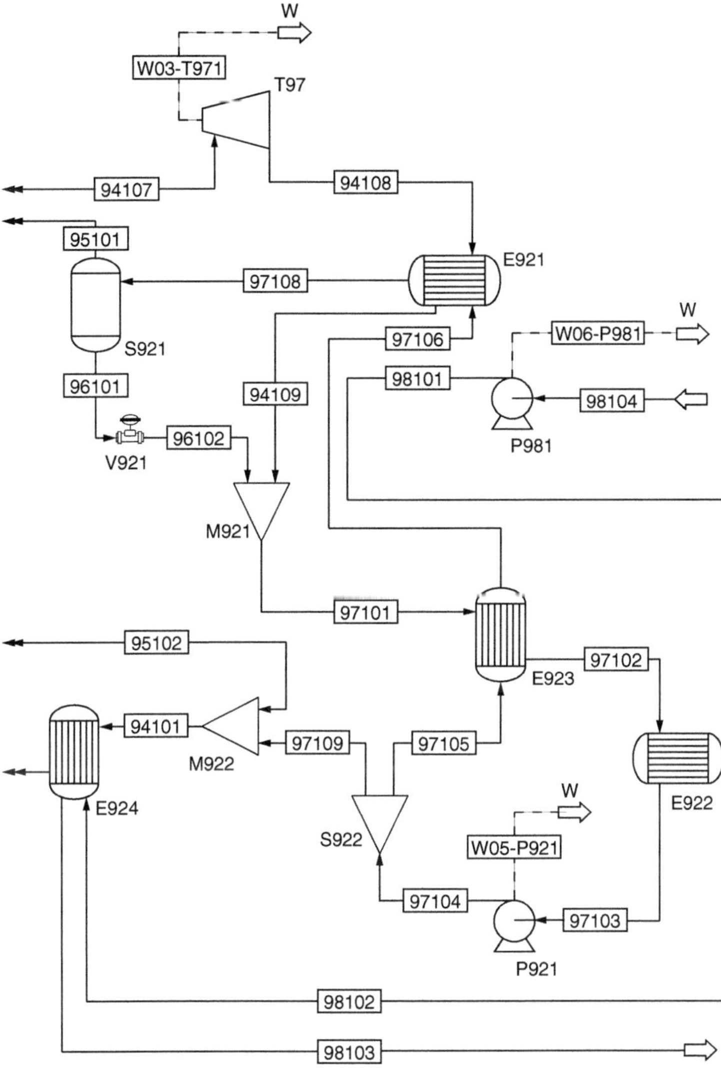

Fig. 1.3 Aspen Plus® flowsheet (2 of 2)

The separator creates two streams of different NH_3/H_2O concentrations, given by the composition of the vapour and liquid in the pressure-point temperature at the inlet of the separator. The liquid flow (stream 96101) serves to deplete the ammonia concentration of the working fluid from Regenerator I (stream 94109) and facilitate condensation. Before both streams are to be mixed (94109 at the outlet of Regenerator I and 96102), a valve (V921) adjusts the liquid reflux pressure (stream 96101), resulting in stream 96102 which is involved in the mix.

The separated gaseous stream (stream 95101) passes through Regenerator III (E925), being an input flow of the recovery boiler. After passing through Regenerator III, the gaseous stream (stream 95102) is newly mixed with the main flow (stream 97109) to restore the initial NH_3/H_2O concentration in stream 94101.

The stream with the original mixture (stream 94101) from the boiler passes through the high temperature Condenser II (E924) to recover the saturated liquid state (stream 94102). Due to pump 2 (P922), the maximum's pressure of the cycle is obtained. Finally, the working fluid (stream 94103) passes through Regenerator III (E925) before entering (stream 94104) the boiler.

1.3 Simulation and System Parametrisation

For the proposed cycle, it is necessary to have thermodynamic data of the streams and substances present in the process. To perform thermoeconomic analysis throughout this book, the mentioned electricity generation system has been simulated in Aspen Plus®, using the thermoeconomic data obtained by the aforementioned as data from the different matter streams: mass flow, temperature, pressure, composition, molecular mass, enthalpy and entropy. The enthalpy and entropy of the streams with the same composition are also obtained, considering that they are at ambient temperature and pressure [1].

Figures 1.2 and 1.3 show the flowsheet of the simulation performed with Aspen Plus®. Outgoing exhaust gases from the compressor station gas turbine (stream 93103) pass through three heat exchangers (simulating the heat recovery steam generator) prior to being emitted into the atmosphere.

The gas turbine is located within the compressor station, so therefore it is not part of the analysed process. The process suggested makes use of the exhaust gases from the turbine. This turbine will remain untouched in order to ensure that the compression station functionality remains the same. It is important that any energy improvement suggested is not only profitable, but guarantees the original facility normal operation and production from not been deteriorated by the alternative proposed. Only the composition, mass flow, temperature and pressure of the gases at the entrance to the boiler are taken into account.

In Figs. 1.2 and 1.3, it can be seen that all the heat and work currents have been simulated as outgoing, although in some pieces of equipment in the real process the currents go in the opposite direction. All heat and work currents have been identified by the letters Q and W, followed by a number. This criteria has a twofold objective: firstly, it makes this type of currents easy to identify and secondly, it forces Aspen Plus® to calculate their value during the simulation [2]. If currents are represented with their real direction in the case of ingoing currents their characteristics must be provided to the simulator (value, temperature, etc...). By putting the currents, as outputs, the program calculates the value of these flows.

The real direction (ingoing or outgoing) of these flows is given by the criterion of signs used by Aspen Plus®. The values given for work and heat flows are positive when they are inputs, so if the value of the work produced by a power generator (turbine) is calculated, Aspen Plus® will give it a negative sign. The same criterion is applied by Aspen Plus® to heat flows.

So the correct direction of the heat and work flows and their value can be obtained numerically by observing the signs and values calculated by the simulator. This criterion should be consistent with the purpose of the piece of equipment under analysis.

The heat recovery system is simulated using three heat exchangers (E914, E914 and E915) and the steam turbine system is simulated using T971. The condensers are simulated by E924 and E922 (LP condenser), being pump P981 the water pump of this system.

To simplify the study of the system, it has been divided into two different subsystems, as shown in Figs. 1.2 and 1.3, which physically correspond to the heat recovery system (Fig. 1.2) and the cascade condensation and turbine system as a whole (Fig. 1.3).

`Workbook WB1001` (Annex A) contains the data collected from the simulation organized in three sheets: matter streams, work streams, and heat streams. All calculations and results of the analysis of the process as a whole, with the minimum level of aggregation, are included. In this analysis each piece of equipment and current shown in Figs. 1.2 and 1.3 is studied. This information can be found in the website of this book, and references will be given along the book for each precise calculation or result.

This makes easier not only the reading of this book but the comprehension of the analysis, calculations, results and the process. If the reader is interested in having the details of a particular part of the analysis (or the analysis as a whole), ancillary additional information can be consulted in the website of the book. The use of the MHBT tool [3] applied to the sample process analyzed in the book will be included as part of the ancillary information that can be found in Annex A and on the website.

References

1. Hiendrink AP (1996) Exergy analysis with a flowsheeting simulator. I. Theory; calculating exergies of material streams. Chem Eng Sci 51(20):4693–4700
2. Khoshnoodi M (1997) Simulation of partial oxidation of natural gas to synthesis gas using Aspen. Fuel Process Technol 50:257–289
3. Querol E, Gonzalez-Regueral B, Perez-Benedito JL (2011) Novel application for exergy and thermoeconomic analysis of processes simulated with Aspen Plus®. Energy 36:964–974
4. Valero A, Lozano MA, Serra L (1994) CGAM problem: definition and conventional solution. Energy 19(3):279–286

Chapter 2
Exergy Concept and Determination

Abstract Exergy is the cornerstone of exergetic and thermoeconomic analyses. This chapter explains what exergy is and how to calculate it for matter, heat, and work flows. The calculations depend on the information available, but it is easy to obtain at least an approximation. The example case is used briefly (normal text) and in detailed form (grey boxes).

2.1 Introduction

The exergy of a portion of matter is equal to the maximum useful work obtainable when taken from its given state to the thermodynamic equilibrium with the environment, without intervention rather than its own and the one of the environment [7]. Such a final state of equilibrium is known as dead state. From another point of view, the exergy can be considered as a measure of the existing disequilibrium between the considered matter and the environment.

To be able to carry out exergy calculations, it is necessary to define a reasonable idealized model for the environment, which is taken as reference, since the exergy will always depend on the system's and environment's states. It is also essential to analyse the diverse possibilities of reaching the dead state of equilibrium with the environment, following the restrictions imposed on the different analysed systems.

The exergy of every energy flow (matter flow, heat, work,...) can be calculated with the methods shown in this chapter, as it is explained. A very important point will be the analysis of the destruction of exergy due to the inevitable irreversibility of real processes.

2.2 Environment and Dead State

From a theoretical standpoint, the environment must be in thermodynamic equilibrium, and therefore with no usable energy, but in fact it is not, as its intensive properties vary from place to place and from time to time. Owing to a high activation

E. Querol et al., *Practical Approach to Exergy and Thermoeconomic Analyses of Industrial Processes*, SpringerBriefs in Energy,
DOI: 10.1007/978-1-4471-4622-3_2,

energy, many reactions—thermodynamically spontaneous—that lead to thermodynamic equilibrium are kinetically blocked. A very important and noticeable case is that of molecular nitrogen contained in atmospheric air and dissolved in oceanic waters. In presence of oxygen or water, the dissolved gaseous nitric acid in the atmosphere, and the dissolved nitrate ion in seawater, are more stable. The free enthalpies of formation of nitric acid and of nitrates are negative, and therefore their formation reactions are spontaneous. The energetic barrier that stops them is the rupture of the triple bond of the nitrogen molecule, which has an activation energy of almost 1 000 kJ mol^{-1}. At ordinary temperatures, the reaction speeds are practically zero. To produce them, really high temperatures are needed, which can be given in combustion processes or in atmospheric electric discharges. Owing to this—as we shall see promptly—atmospheric nitrogen is used as a reference substance and not as a proper stable compound.

In fact, the usable energy of the natural environment is not null, since useful work would be possible to obtain if it evolves towards thermodynamic equilibrium. Therefore, it is vital to compromise in the formulation of a model that approximates the real ambient environment and is thermodynamically acceptable. A conventional stable reference environment (SRE) is established, normally at $T_o = 298.15$ K (25 °C) and $p_o = 1$ atm (1.013 bar), due to the fact that most of the thermodynamic properties are tabulated at this T_o, p_o [16].

The calculation of thermodynamic properties of substances requires a clear and unambiguous characterization of thermodynamic states. The normal or standard state of a certain substance at a generic temperature T is defined as the most stable pure form of that component at this temperature and at a normal pressure of 1 atm, which is usually the SRE one (called AER in the MHBT software [11]).

The values of the properties in the *standard state* are distinguished with the superscript °. The basic data tabulation is usually done at the conventional temperature of 25 °C, equivalent to 298.15 K, called *normal temperature*, usually being that of the SRE. The normal state at 298.15 K is commonly called the *normal state*, leaving the explicit indication of the temperature for those who take a different one.

This is the reason why the subscript ° has been used in this text to identify a temperature of 25 °C and a pressure of 1 atm for the SRE.

Chemically the SRE is formed by diverse existent reference substances in the natural environment, to which null exergy is assigned and possesses the following properties:

- Approximates as much as possible to thermodynamic equilibrium.
- Reproduces reality reasonably.
- Is large enough so that its exchanges of matter and energy with systems under study do not alter significantly its intensive properties (temperature, pressure and chemical potential).

The SRE is used as a common reference level for exergy determination. In any case, this is indispensable to ensure consistent calculations. When the system under study reaches complete thermodynamic equilibrium with the environment, it is assumed that it is already in the dead state. In this state, pressure, temperature and chemical potential of the system are equal to that of the environment.

Closed systems cannot achieve total equilibrium with the environment, as matter exchanges, which are probably needed to reach chemical equilibrium, are not allowed. In this case, a state of physical or restricted equilibrium is achieved, in which only pressure and temperature match, which we will know as environmental state.

The natural environment can be considered to be made up of three subsystems that, strictly speaking, are not entirely in thermodynamic equilibrium, neither in internal equilibrium nor between themselves. These are the following:

- *Atmosphere*: Saturated humid air, in equilibrium with liquid water. Provides reference substances: oxygen, nitrogen, as well as the other gases that make up the air including CO_2, which is the reference substance for carbon.
- *Hydrosphere*: Saturated liquid water (H_2O), which is a reference substance for hydrogen.
- *Lithosphere*: The reference substances are selected from those most abundant and of lowest value, existing in the solid crust. For example, for sulphur and calcium, gypsum ($CaSO_4 \cdot 2H_2O$) and calcite ($CaCO_3$) are respectively taken.

This SRE model closely approximates the real environment, and therefore conserves most of the existing imbalances in it. For example, for nitrogen, the reference substance chosen is the one in the atmosphere, resulting in normal negative exergy for sodium, potassium and calcium nitrates.

2.3 Physical Exergy

The physical exergy b_{ph} is the maximum useful work obtained by passing the unit of mass of a substance of the generic state (T, p) to the environmental (T_o, p_o) state through purely physical processes [1, 3, 17]. Thus, if kinetic and potential energy are not taken into consideration, according to Eq. 2.1, the physical exergy b_{ph} can be determined with the enthalpy and entropy values of the stream (characterized by its composition), both at the generic state, and the environmental state temperatures and pressures.

$$b_{ph} = [h(T, p) - h(T_o, p_o)] - T_o\,[s(T, p) - s(T_o, p_o)] \tag{2.1}$$

For the determination of physical exergy, always using (2.1), there are two methods that can be used, based on the data available. The *direct method* involves the direct use of the values of enthalpy and entropy, which shall be known, (i.e. with the simulation of the process). Whenever there exists reliable entropy and enthalpy data in terms of temperature and pressure, its direct input is preferable, to achieve more accurate results with less effort.

As the $h(T_o, p_o)$ and $s(T_o, p_o)$ are the values of enthalpy and entropy at T_o, p_o, they will be referred to in the text as h_o and s_o. If the values are not known, then they can be estimated to obtain an approximate value of the physical exergy, also using (2.1).

2.3.1 Direct Method

If data concerning enthalpy and entropy in terms of temperature and pressure is available, Eq. 2.1 provides the values of physical exergy. When analysing facilities, all the streams with equal composition have the same h_o and s_o values [8].

In the simulation used the enthalpy and entropy data is given, but it is simple to obtain the specific values of enthalpy and entropy in thermo-physical equilibrium (same T and p) of the SRE [9].

Firstly, all the streams of equal composition are identified with the same first three digits, as shown in Figs. 1.2 and 1.3. Streams with equal composition, can only be differentiated amongst themselves in terms of the temperature, pressure and mass flow of each stream, but all of them will have the same thermodynamic intensive properties if the same temperature and pressure is given to them, as it will happen at T_o, p_o.

Secondly, as shown in Figs. 1.2 and 1.3, for each different stream composition in the simulation, there has been added a pair of streams joined by a heater, one entering and the other one exiting the heater. The purpose is to give the incoming stream the chemical composition of the fluid, in order to obtain in the exiting stream the thermodynamic intensive properties of every stream with the same composition at T_o, p_o. Thus, the incoming stream is identified with letter Z, the exiting stream with the letters SRE, and the heater with the letters SRE, all of them followed by the same three digits identifying streams of identical composition.

Due to the existence of six different compositions or fluids in the case analysed, streams beginning with: 931, 941, 951, 961, 971, 981, six streams have been brought to the stable reference state using the streams: Z931, Z941, Z951, Z961, Z971 and Z981. The data of the currents analyzed (931, 341, 951, 961, 971, 981) can be directly introduced in the Z streams (Z931, Z941, Z951, Z961, Z971, Z981) or transferred to them by using specific functions in Aspen Plus®. The mass flow chosen in these currents does not matter as only specific values of enthalpy and entropy in the SRE are going to be used, being the same for the current that has the same composition.

The "Z-streams" are used as inputs of the heaters: SRE931, SRE941, SRE951, SRE961, SRE971, SRE981, followed by the outgoing streams, named exactly the same as the heaters constituting their source: SRE931, SRE941, SRE951, SRE961, SRE971. The input streams of these heaters are only used to receive the chemical input data of each stream from the simulation.

The heaters are configured to give their exiting streams the temperature and pressure of the SRE: T_o, p_o. Thus, the exiting streams have the chemical composition of each stream of the process at the temperature and pressure of the SRE, providing the thermodynamic intensive properties needed to calculate the physical exergy (see Sect. 2.3.1).

With the method explained, the $h(T_\text{o}, p_\text{o})$ and $s(T_\text{o}, p_\text{o})$ values of every stream correspond to the specific enthalpy and entropy values calculated by the simulator for the stream identified with the letters SRE, followed by the three digits identifying the same composition.

Table 2.1 Data selection for the physical exergy calculation of E914 streams from the data obtained in the simulation

Streams	93103	93104	SRE931	94106	94107	SRE941
$\dot{n}$	1.48	1.48		0.47	0.47	
$\dot{m}$	42.08	42.08		8.20	8.20	
T [°C]	500.00	442.47		255.66	350.00	
p [bar]	1.06	1.06		115.00	115.00	
x	1.00	1.00		1.00	1.00	
$\tilde{h}$	−9 966.81	−11 826.94	−25 985.90	−118 100.00	−112 270.00	−143 310.00
h	−349.54	−414.77	−911.33	−6 782.92	−6 448.21	−8 230.68
$\tilde{s}$	32 660.97	30 161.05	−554.96	−97 622.99	−87 439.36	−137 110.00
s	1 145.42	1 057.75	−19.46	−5 606.94	−5 022.04	−7 874.61
Mole frac						
H_2O	0.0550	0.0550	0.0550	0.3865	0.3865	0.3865
NH_3	0.0000	0.0000	0.0000	0.6135	0.6135	0.6135
CO_2	0.0288	0.0288	0.0288	0.0000	0.0000	0.0000
CH_4	0.0000	0.0000	0.0000	0.0000	0.0000	0.0000
C_2H_6	0.0000	0.0000	0.0000	0.0000	0.0000	0.0000
C_3H_8	0.0000	0.0000	0.0000	0.0000	0.0000	0.0000
C_4H_{10}	0.0000	0.0000	0.0000	0.0000	0.0000	0.0000
C_5H_{12}	0.0000	0.0000	0.0000	0.0000	0.0000	0.0000
O_2	0.1479	0.1479	0.1479	0.0000	0.0000	0.0000
N_2	0.7683	0.7683	0.7683	0.0000	0.0000	0.0000

For a piece of equipment with no chemical processes (reactions, separation or mixtures of substances), only the physical exergy of the streams needs to be calculated, because the composition of the incoming and outgoing streams is identical.

In the case under study, the heat exchanger E914 is an example of a piece of equipment without chemical processes. This piece of equipment can be seen in different ways:

- In a material vision, streams 93103 and 94106 enter and streams 93104 and 94107 exit the heat exchanger.
- In an energetic vision, fluid 931 losses temperature and enthalpy, giving it to the heat exchanger, where the fluid 941 increases its temperature and enthalpy. If the heat exchanger is well insulated it can be said that the energy given by one fluid is completely received by the other.
- Finally, in an exergetic vision, the fluid 931 gives exergy to the heat exchanger, which is used to increase the exergy of stream 941, but only partially. The exergy given by fluid 931 is higher than the exergy received by stream 941, which means that some of the exergy has been destroyed inside the equipment, in a non-recoverable way.

For the calculation of the physical exergy of the aforesaid streams, the SRE streams with the same composition have to be considered: SRE931 and SRE941. Upon

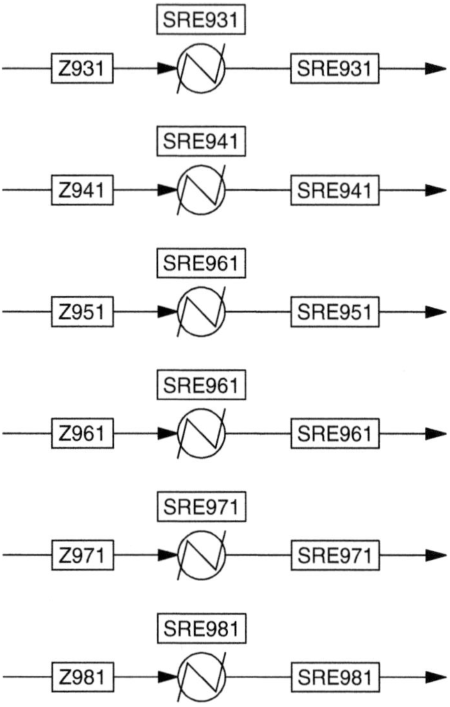

Fig. 2.1 Simulation of the SRE using Aspen Plus®

completion of the simulation, the mass and molar flow data is obtained, as well as the enthalpy and entropy in terms of pressure and temperature, so it is possible to directly calculate the exergy of the streams under analysis. Table 2.1 shows the data from the above mentioned, obtained from the simulation. The specific values of the SRE stream: SRE941, provides the values of h_o and s_o for streams 94106 and 94107, as all of them share the same fluid composition 941. The same happens with streams 93103, 93104 and SRE931 (Fig. 2.1).

The calculation of the exergy of the streams using (2.1), gives the specific physical exergy in a mass base b. This calculation can also be realized in a molar base. In either case, the resulting value must be multiplied by the mass or molar flows respectively, to obtain the value of $\dot{B}_{ph}$ provided in Table 2.2.

As shown in Table 2.2, the use of either base (molar or mass) offers very similar values (Tables 2.3 and 2.4 show an explanaition of the content of each row and the calculations done in `WB1001`).

The calculations for the whole process are very similar. With the aid of the stream identification used and the workbook functions, they are quite easy to do. The calculations have been performed in the sheet `BCorrM` from `WB1011` (Annex A). In this sheet, firstly, a selection is realized from the data contained in the `m`, `W`, `Q` sheets from `WB1001`:

Table 2.2 Physical exergy of E914 streams

Streams	93103	93104	94106	94107
$\dot{m}$	42.08	42.08	8.20	8.20
$h - h_o$	561.79	496.56	1447.76	1782.47
$s - s_o$	1.16	1.08	2.27	2.85
b_{ph}	214.48	175.38	771.66	931.98
$\dot{B}_{ph}$	9 025.33	7 380.20	6 328.62	7 643.51
n	1.48	1.48	0.47	0.47
$h - h_o$	16 019.09	14 158.96	25 210.00	31 040.00
$s - s_o$	33.22	30.72	39.49	49.67
b_{ph}	6 115.76	5 000.98	13 436.95	16 230.70
$\dot{B}_{ph}$	9 025.33	7 380.20	6 329.36	7 645.33
Difference				
Absolute [kW]	0.00	0.00	0.74	1.82
Relative [%]	0.00	0.00	0.01	0.02

Table 2.3 Identification of content and row in `WB1001`

Row	Content
1	Stream identification
2	Equipment where the streams enters
3	Equipment from which the streams come from
4	Temperature
5	Pressure
6	Mass flow
7	Enthalpy given by the simulator
10	Specific enthalpy
11	Specific entropy
21	Molecular weight
22–32	Composition of the streams in molar fraction

Several calculations are made and added to this sheet to enable a quick vision of all the thermodynamic stream data of interest.

The `29` matter streams of the case occupy columns `A` to `AD`. Columns `AE` to `AJ` are occupied with the information of the six SRE streams: SRE931, SRE941, SRE951, SRE961, SRE971, SRE981, providing with their specific enthalpy (`row 10`) and specific entropy (`row 11`) data, h_o and s_o values of all the

Table 2.4 Example of calculations done and shown in `WB1001`

Row	Content
8	Positive enthalpy. This row is the specific positive enthalpy times the mass flow. The calculation is: `row 17` × `row 6`
9	Total exergy of the stream
12	Specific enthalpy at T_o, $p_o(h_o)$. Data read from the specific enthalpy (`row 10`) of the corresponding SRE stream
13	Specific entropy at T_o, $p_o(s_o)$. Data read from the specific enthalpy (`row 11`) of the corresponding SRE stream
14	Specific enthalpy difference between the stream state and the T_o, p_o value: `row 10` − `row 12`
15	Specific entropy difference between the stream T, p and the T_o, p_o value: `row 11` − `row 13`
16	Specific high heating value, calculated for each stream making use of the data composition and the tabulated HHV of the substances present in the simulation
17	Specific positive enthalpy. This row is added to obtain positive values of enthalpy. The value contained is the difference between the enthalpy given by the simulator (`row 7`) and H_o, summed all it with the HHV. The calculation is: `row 14 + row 16`
18	Specific physical exergy (b_{ph}). Calculated according to Eq. 2.1, where $T_o = 298.15$ K. The calculation is: (`row 14` − `298.15` × `row 15`)
19	Specific chemical exergy (b_{ch}). Calculated according to Eq. 2.24
20	Specific total exergy (b)

Table 2.5 High heating values of the substances present in the simulation

Substance	HHV
H_2O	0
NH_3	382 800
CO_2	0
CH_4	890 700
C_2H_6	1 560 700
C_3H_8	2 219 200
C_4H_{10}	2 877 500
C_5H_{12}	3 535 400
O_2	0
N_2	0

streams with same composition. As it can be shown, the molar composition (`rows 22` and below) are identical between the streams with the same first 3 numbers in their names, so for this task an excel function can be used, that compares them and search for the adequate values in `rows 10` and `11` of the corresponding SRE stream (this is not done in the workbook).

As the HHV of the streams depends exclusively in the composition of the streams and the HHV values of the substances (see Table 2.5), the HHV obtained for each SRE stream is also the HHV value for all the streams with same composition. Thus, in the range `AE16:AJ16`, the value of the specific HHV (in kJ $kmol^{-1}$) of the fluids has been calculated, making use of the composition (`rows 23–32`) and the HHV of the substances in the same order, available in `rows 33–42` (in kJ $kmol^{-1}$).

2.3.2 Indirect Method

In the case that the enthalpy and entropy data is unavailable, the enthalpy and entropy differences of Eq. 2.1 must be formulated for the specific substance under study. Considering the two particular cases that occur more frequently, depending on whether it involves an incompressible substance or an ideal gas.

2.3.2.1 Incompressible Condensed Substance (Pure or Homogeneous Mixture)

The enthalpy and the entropy term must be calculated. As for the enthalpy, upon developing s in terms of T and p, Eq. 2.2 remains:

$$\begin{aligned} \mathrm{d}h &= T\left[\left(\frac{\partial s}{\partial T}\right)_p \mathrm{d}T + \left(\frac{\partial s}{\partial p}\right)_T \mathrm{d}p\right] + v\mathrm{d}p \\ &= T\left(\frac{\partial s}{\partial T}\right)_p \mathrm{d}T + \left[v + T\left(\frac{\partial s}{\partial p}\right)_T\right]\mathrm{d}p \end{aligned} \tag{2.2}$$

As the last member expresses $\mathrm{d}h$ in terms of $\mathrm{d}T$ and $\mathrm{d}p$, the coefficient of its first term must be equal to the specific heat at constant pressure c_p [1]. Additionally applying Maxwell's formula to the $\left(\frac{\partial s}{\partial p}\right)_T$ of the second term, it gives (2.3):

$$\mathrm{d}h = c_p\mathrm{d}T + \left[v - T\left(\frac{\partial v}{\partial T}\right)_p\right]\mathrm{d}p \tag{2.3}$$

For a condensed body, $\left(\frac{\partial v}{\partial T}\right)_p$ can be neglected, so that very approximately in this case, the following is verified:

$$\mathrm{d}h = c_p\mathrm{d}T + v\mathrm{d}p \tag{2.4}$$

The entropic term is deduced to be in general:

$$ds = \frac{1}{T}dh - \frac{v}{T}dp \quad (2.5)$$

Applying (2.4) obtained by applying Maxwell's function to a condensed body in (2.3):

$$ds = c_p \frac{dT}{T} \quad (2.6)$$

Integrating both expressions between the states (T_o, p_o) and (T, p) and expressing c_p in terms of T, the following dimensionless polynomial, named a "NASA polynomial", is obtained for the molar heat $\tilde{c}_p$:

$$\frac{\tilde{c}_p^o(T)}{\tilde{R}} = a_1 + a_2T + a_3T^2 + a_4T^3 + a_5T^4 \quad (2.7)$$

where $\tilde{R}$ is the gas constant, and $a_1, \ldots, a_5$ are constants corresponding to the considered substance. There are different data bases for these coefficients and their validity interval for diverse substances.

Specific heat $\tilde{c}_p$ is easily computed with the following expression:

$$c_p = \frac{\tilde{c}_p}{M} \quad (2.8)$$

M represents the *molar mass* of the substance. In small enough temperature intervals, c_p can be considered constant; in these cases the physical exergy can be calculated roughly as follows:

$$b_{ph} = c_p (T - T_o) - T_o c_p \ln \frac{T}{T_o} + v(p - p_o) \quad (2.9)$$

In general, this expression provides enough approximation for small temperature and pressure intervals.

2.3.2.2 Ideal Gaseous Substance (Pure or of Constant Composition)

The enthalpy of an ideal gas only depends on its temperature so that the enthalpy increase is simply:

$$h - h_o = \int_{T_o}^{T} c_p dT \quad (2.10)$$

As for the entropy, it is expressed through (2.11), where R is the gas constant:

$$s - s_o = \int_{T_o}^{T} c_p \frac{\mathrm{d}T}{T} - R \int_{p_o}^{p} \frac{\mathrm{d}p}{p} = \int_{T_o}^{T} c_p \frac{\mathrm{d}T}{T} - R \ln \frac{p}{p_o} \tag{2.11}$$

If c_p is considered to be constant, the physical exergy can be expressed by (2.12):

$$b_{ph} = c_p (T - T_o) - T_o c_p \ln \frac{T}{T_o} + RT_o \ln \frac{p}{p_o} \tag{2.12}$$

If the gaseous substance is liquid at T_o, p_o (in the SRE), then the enthalpy of vaporization Δh_{vap} must be added to Eq. 2.10, and the corresponding term $\frac{\Delta h_{\mathrm{vap}}}{T_{\mathrm{vap}}}$ must be added to Eq. 2.11. If the gaseous substance is a subcooled liquid in the SRE then, the enthalpy and entropy increases from (T_o, p_o) to the boiling point must be added, following the Sect. 2.3.2.1 procedure, then the vaporization shall be considered, and finally the Eqs. 2.10 and 2.11 for the gaseous temperature and pressure increases shall be considered. Due to the Hess law, in this case, the path followed from the (T_o, p_o) to reach the final state at (T, p) of the streams are all equivalent. Nevertheless, special attention should be given to the vaporization stage, as the values of Δh_{vap} and T_{vap} depend on the pressure of the boiling point selected.

2.4 Chemical Exergy

Chemical exergy is the maximum useful energy which would be attained by passing from the environmental state to the dead state, by means of chemical processes with reactants and products at the environmental temperature and pressure, when the stream composition is not in chemical equilibrium with the environment.

If the substance of a stream is present in the environment but in a partial pressure greater than the one it has in the environment, some work can still be done in the expansion of this component. For example, if a stream composed exclusively of CO_2 at (T_o, p_o), is considered, the stream has no physical exergy, but as CO_2 is only a small fraction of the air composition (0.035 %), the pressure decrease of the stream from p_o to the partial pressure of CO_2 in the environment, can theoretically produce work, and this will also be called chemical exergy, although no chemical reaction is produced.

If the chemical exergy of any of the substances of the process is unknown (not available in tables), they can be determined through two methods:

- General Method: calculating the chemical exergy of the chemical elements which constitute the substance and the free energy of formation of the substance.

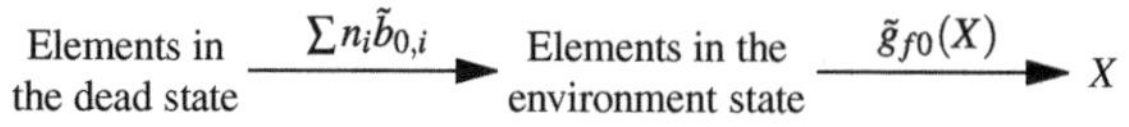

Fig. 2.2 Formation process of a substance from its elements in the dead state

- Alternative Method: when the substance is not found in the SRE but is stoichiometrically linked to substances contained in the SRE and only to them.

In any case, once the chemical exergy of all the components is calculated, the chemical exergy of the stream can be calculated, according to the instructions given in Sect. 2.5.3.

2.5 Chemical Exergy of Substances

2.5.1 General Method

We will consider a compound X, formed by various elements whose chemical exergy $\tilde{b}_{0,i}$ is known. Evidently, the chemical exergy of X will be equal to the minimum useful work required to form it from its elements in the dead state, through the process shown in Fig. 2.2, where $\tilde{g}_{f0}(X)$ represents the free energy of formation of X, supposing that the normal state is the same as the environmental one:

Therefore, the total is equivalent to the chemical exergy of X, as follows:

$$\tilde{b}_{ch}(X) = \sum n_i \tilde{b}_{ch,i}\,(\text{elems.}) + \tilde{g}_{f0}(X) \tag{2.13}$$

CO_2 can be found in streams 93103 and 93104. Although its normal chemical exergy is tabulated, this method will be applied to calculate it as an example. According to Eq. 2.14, the chemical exergy of CO_2 can be written as:

$$\tilde{b}_{ch}(CO_2) = \tilde{b}_{ch}(C) + \tilde{b}_{ch}(O_2) + \tilde{g}_{f0}(CO_2) \tag{2.14}$$

Using the values of normalized chemical exergy, as well as of free energy, the following result is obtained:

$$\tilde{b}_{ch}(CO_2) = 410\,820 + 4\,000 - 394\,400 = 20\,420\,\text{kJ kmol}^{-1} \tag{2.15}$$

The difference with the tabulated value is of 1.5 %, this being considered acceptable.

2.5.2 Alternative Method

This method will be used in the cases in which the substance cannot be found in the SRE, but is stoichiometrically linked to substances only from the SRE. Assuming that the reaction that links them is written in the standard form where the negative coefficients v_i correspond to the positive reactants and the positive ones to the reaction products:

$$\sum_{\forall i} v_i C_i = 0 \tag{2.16}$$

For this reaction at T_o and p_o (2.17) is verified, which represents $-W_{u,\max.}$, which is the minimum useful work required for a reaction to take place.

$$\Delta B_{\text{react.}} = \sum_{\forall i} v_i \tilde{b}_{ch,i} \tag{2.17}$$

Equation (2.18) is also verified, where $\tilde{g}_{f0,i}$ represents the standard free energy of formation of the generic substance at T_o and p_o.

$$-W_{u,\max.} = \Delta G_{\text{react.}} = \sum_{\forall i} v_i \tilde{g}_{f0,i} \tag{2.18}$$

Therefore, from expressions (2.17) and (2.18) the following expression can be written:

$$\sum_{\forall i} v_i (\tilde{b}_{ch,i} - \tilde{g}_{f0,i}) = 0. \tag{2.19}$$

If substance j does not belong to the SRE and its chemical exergy is the one to be calculated, (2.19) can be written as (2.20)

$$v_j (\tilde{b}_{ch,j} - \tilde{g}_{f0,j}) + \sum_{i \neq j} v_i (\tilde{b}_{ch,i} - \tilde{g}_{f0,i}) = 0. \tag{2.20}$$

Reordering (2.20), the sought chemical exergy is determined with (2.21).

$$\tilde{b}_{ch,j} = \tilde{g}_{f0,j} - \frac{1}{v_j} \sum_{i \neq j} v_i (\tilde{b}_{ch,i} - \tilde{g}_{f0,i}) \tag{2.21}$$

We will apply (2.21) to the case of CH_4, it does not belong to the SRE but verifies reaction (2.22) which links it to SRE substances:

$$CH_4(g) + 2O_2(g) = CO_2(g) + 2H_2O(g) \tag{2.22}$$

From the equation of reaction (2.22) and the data tables, the information in Table 2.6 is obtained.

Table 2.6 Chemical exergy and standard free energy of formation

Substance	ν_i	$\tilde{g}_{fo,i}$	$\tilde{b}_{ch,i}$
CH_4	−1	−50 757	?
O_2	−2	0	3 970
CO_2	+1	−394 364	20 140
H_2O	+2	−237 141	3 120

Table 2.7 Chemical exergy of the substances present in the simulation

Substance	$\tilde{b}_{ch}$
H_2O	3 120
NH_3	341 250
CO_2	20 140
CH_4	836 510
C_2H_6	1 504 360
C_3H_8	2 163 190
C_4H_{10}	2 818 930
C_2H_{12}	3 477 050
O_2	3 970
N_2	720

With the help of (2.21) we can write (2.23).

$$\tilde{b}_{ch}(CH_4) = -\,50\ 757 - (1/-1)[-2(3\ 970 - 0) + 1(20\ 140 + 394\ 364) + 2(3\ 120 + 237\ 141)] = 836\ 329\,\text{kJ kmol}^{-1} \quad (2.23)$$

This result compared with data contained in other databases has an error of 0.02 %. This method is very useful for fuels whose chemical exergy is not available in tables.

Unlike the case of physical exergy, the data necessary for the calculation of chemical exergy cannot be directly obtained from the performed simulation, from which the data relative to the composition of the different streams will be used. The normalized chemical exergy per mole of the components of the streams is obtained through the process described in Sect. 2.5.1 obtaining the value of the chemical exergy of the different components at 1 atm and 298.15 K in Table 2.7.

2.5.3 Chemical Exergy of a Stream

Once the chemical exergy of all the substances present in the process is known, the chemical exergy of the streams can be evaluated. As the specific chemical exergy depends exclusively on the composition of the streams, it can be calculated only once per composition.

For the calculation of the chemical exergy of a stream, the chemical exergy of its components and their molar fraction must be known. The components of the streams which are part of the SRE, and several others can be found tabulated in [12, 14, 15].

Table 2.8 Specific and total chemical exergy of E914 streams

Streams	93103	93104	94106	94107
$\dot{m}$	42.08	42.08	8.20	8.20
b_{ch}	66.37	66.37	12 094.44	12 094.44
$\dot{B}_{ch}$	2 792.75	2 792.75	2 792.75	2 792.75

In this case, the chemical exergy of the stream is calculated as [4]:

$$\tilde{b}_{ch} = \sum x_i \tilde{b}_{ch,i} \tag{2.24}$$

It is important to point out that in other publications [7], the formula given for the chemical exergy determination is slightly different. For both gas mixtures and ideal liquid solutions, formula (2.25) is applied:

$$\tilde{b}_{ch} = \sum x_i \tilde{b}_{ch,i} + \tilde{R}T_o \sum x_i \ln x_i \tag{2.25}$$

The difference between both equations is $\tilde{R}T_o \sum x_i \ln x_i$, which account for the exergy destroyed ($\ln x_i$ is always negative) due to the mixing of the different components of the stream (it can be called *mixture exergy*). As can be seen in comparison with the term $RT_o \ln \frac{p}{p_o}$ for the physical exergy (2.12), this term corresponds to $s - s_o$, and comes from the consideration of the partial pressure of each component in the numerator; which is $x_i p_o$ in the SRE according to Dalton's Law. The use of (2.24) or (2.25) depends on the pressure used in (2.12). If the partial pressure of each component is used in (2.12), or the entropy used is the entropy of the stream, then the mixing effect is already considered, and therefore the appropriate equation is (2.24), in any other case Eq. 2.25 must be used.

This expresses the chemical exergy of the mixture in terms of its components and of its composition [16]. Upon obtaining the exergy of the components that form the streams under analysis as well as its compositions attained from the simulation, the chemical exergy of the different streams that affect E914 can be obtained. Table 2.8 shows the acquired results, both unit chemical exergy and each stream's chemical exergy:

This method has been used to obtain the chemical exergy of the six different compositions present in the case analyzed, present in the SRE streams.

In the worksheet `BCorrM` of the workbook `WB1011` the chemical exergy of the substances present in the composition are written in the range `AE43:AE52` in kJ kmol^{-1}. With these values, the chemical compositions given in `rows 23-32`, and the molecular weight available in row 21, the specific chemical exergy is calculated, for each SRE stream, in the range `AE19:AJ19`, applying Eq. 2.24 (which gives the result in kJ kmol^{-1}) divided by the molecular weight [kg kmol^{-1}] given in `row 21` (to obtain the value in kJ kg^{-1} instead of kJ kmol^{-1}). As all the streams in the simulation have the same composition as that of one of the SRE streams, the specific calculated values are used for all of them, filling `row 19`.

2.5.4 Chemical Exergy of a Fuel Stream

The determination of the chemical exergy of a fuel is a particular case of the calculation of the chemical exergy of a stream, of great interest in the analysis of industrial facilities.

If the methods already described cannot be used, an approximate determination of the specific chemical exergy of industrial fuels can be easily carried out through empirical coefficients f_l and f_h, which relate it to the lower or higher heating values (2.26), where LHV and HHV respectively represent the lower and higher heating values.

$$\mathrm{b_{ch}} = f_l \cdot \mathrm{LHV} = f_h \cdot \mathrm{HHV} \tag{2.26}$$

This can be done because solid and liquid fuels have usually exergy values similar to the HHV, and gaseous fuels have values very similar to the LHV, so the empirical coefficients are numbers close to 1.

2.6 Total Exergy of a Matter Stream

The calculation of total exergy is usually reduced to the sum of the chemical and physical exergy, including only in specific cases, the kinetic and potential exergy (the energy and exergy values are the same).

2.6.1 Exergy of an Ideal Gas Mixture

The calculation of total exergy can be accomplished via two equivalent methods:

1. Calculating the chemical exergy $\tilde{b}_{ch}(T_o, p_o)$ of the mixture in environmental state through (2.25). Physical exergy, $\tilde{b}_{ph}(T, p)$ is then calculated with (2.12), referring to the unit of substance of the mixture, using the average $\tilde{c}_p$ of the mixture. Finally, the total exergy $\tilde{b}(T, p)$ of the mixture, is obtained through the addition of $\tilde{b}_{ch}(T_o, p_o)$ and $\tilde{b}_{ph}(T, p)$.

Table 2.9 Total, chemical and physical exergy of E914 streams

Streams	93103	93104	94106	94107
$\dot{m}$	42.08	42.08	8.20	8.20
$h - h_o$	561.79	496.56	1 447.76	1 782.47
$s - s_o$	1.16	1.08	2.27	2.85
b_{ph}	214.48	175.38	771.66	931.98
$\dot{B}_{ph}$	9 025.33	7 380.20	6 328.62	7 643.51
b_{ch}	66.37	66.37	12 094.44	12 094.44
$\dot{B}_{ch}$	2 792.75	2 792.75	99 190.74	99 190.74
b	280.85	241.75	12 866.10	13 026.42
$\dot{B}$	11 818.08	10 172.95	105 519.36	106 834.25

2. The $\tilde{b}_{ph,i}(T, p_i)$ of each gas is calculated with (2.12) and to it its chemical exergy is added $\tilde{b}_{ch,i}(T_o, p_o)$ to achieve the total exergy $\tilde{b}_i(T, p_i)$. The molar exergy of the mixture is obtained as (2.27):

$$\tilde{b}\,(T, p) = \sum x_i \tilde{b}_i\,(T, p_i) \tag{2.27}$$

Table 2.9 shows the total exergy, as well as the exergy value of each component. As the $s - s_o$ of the entire stream takes into consideration the mixture effect, the chemical exergy is given by (2.24).

Exactly the same procedure has been followed in the case analysed (`WB1011`), the specific total exergy of the matter stream is calculated in `row 20` of `sheet BCorrM`, adding up the physical and chemical exergies (`rows 18 and 19` respectively).

2.6.2 Exergy of an Ideal Liquid Solution

The same procedure applied in Sect. 2.6.1 for a mixture of ideal gases should be followed. The chemical exergy can be calculated by applying (2.25), and the physical exergy can be calculated applying (2.9) per mole and with the average $\tilde{c}_v$ of the solution. This average of the solution can be calculated applying (2.28):

$$\tilde{c}_v = \frac{\mathrm{d}\tilde{u}}{\mathrm{d}T} = \sum_i x_i \tilde{c}_{v,i} \tag{2.28}$$

Finally, the total exergy $\tilde{b}(T, p)$ of the mixture is obtained through the addition of $b_{ch}(T_o, p_o)$ and $b_{ph}(T, p)$.

2.7 Exergy of Non-Matter Streams

2.7.1 Exergy of Work

Since exergy is defined as the maximum work potential, a work interaction in energy terms is equivalent in exergy terms. Therefore, the exergy content of a work flow is the amount of work of the flow [18]:

$$\dot{B}_W = \dot{W} \tag{2.29}$$

2.7.2 Exergy of Electricity

As electrical energy (active power) can be fully converted in work, the exergy content of electricity is equivalent to the energy content of work and therefore the energy content of the electrical flow. It can be therefore considered as a particular case of the exergy of a work stream [2]:

$$\dot{B}_W = \dot{W}_e \tag{2.30}$$

2.7.3 Exergy of Heat Flows

The exergy content of a heat flow $\dot{Q}$ at a temperature T is of [13]:

$$\dot{B}_q = \left(1 - \frac{T_o}{T}\right)\dot{Q} \tag{2.31}$$

This means that for the same heat flow, the exergy content is lower when the temperature T is nearer T_o. If $T < T_o$, the exergy flow is opposite to the heat flow, and therefore all heat flow input at a lower temperature than the ambient temperature is equivalent to an exergy output. This exergy output is higher as the temperature in which the heat transmission occurs is lower. This is especially important in cryogenic facilities, where a small heat leakage that is incoming from the ambient to the system, can be responsible of high exergy leakages [6].

2.7.4 Exergy of Solar Radiation

Energy emission of a blackbody is σT^4 in $\mathrm{W/m^2}$ where σ is the Stefan-Boltzmann coefficient. This exergy is the equivalent energy transferred to a sink at $T = 0\,K$.

In this case the Carnot efficiency cannot be used to calculate the exergy of the solar radiation flux σT^4 at a temperature T, as a heat sink at the same temperature is considered [5, 19]. If an infinite amount of Carnot engines producing the maximum amount of work are imagined, all of them working between a heat source at T_i absorbing radiation $T_i + \mathrm{d}T_i$ and emitting radiation at T_i, the maximum amount of work is [19]:

$$W_{\max} = \int_{T_i=T_o}^{T_i=T} 4\sigma T_i^3 \mathrm{d}T \left(1 - \frac{T_o}{T_i}\right) = \sigma(T^4 - T_o^4) - \frac{4}{3} T_o \sigma \left(T^3 - T_o^3\right) \quad (2.32)$$

Being the maximum efficiency relative to the radiation energy [10]:

$$\eta_{\max} = \frac{W_{\max}}{\sigma T^4} = 1 - \frac{4T_o}{3T} + \frac{1}{3}\left(\frac{T_o}{T}\right)^4 \quad (2.33)$$

Its value is always smaller than the Carnot efficiency $\left(1 - \frac{T_o}{T}\right)$.

For practical purposes, the exergy of solar radiation can be calculated as the exergy of a heat source at $T = 6000$ K applying Carnot's efficiency [5]. Additionally, as a first approach, the solar radiation exergy can be considered equivalent to its energy (due to uncertainties in solar insolation data, blackbody deviations, etc.).

References

1. Aspelund A (2007) An extendend pinch analysis and design procedure utilizing pressure base exergy for subambiente cooling. App Therm Eng 27:2633–2649
2. Boonnasa S (2006) Performance improvement of the combined cycle power plant by intake air cooling using an absorption chiller. Energy 31:2036–2046
3. Harvey S (1997) Analysis of a reheat gas turbine cycle with chemical recuperation using aspen. Energy Convers Manag 38(15–17):1671–1679
4. Ihsan B (2004) Thermochemical data of pure substances. Wiley, New York. ISBN 3-527-30993-4
5. Jafiri I, Ershadi A, Najafpour E, Hedayat N (2011) Energy and exergy analysis of dual purpose solar collector. Acad Sci Technol 81:259–261
6. Kanoglu M (2001) Cryogenic turbine efficiencies. Exergy Int J 1(3):202–208
7. Kotas TJ (1995) The exergy method of thermal plant analysis. Krieger Publishing Company, Malabar
8. Lie ABK (1994) ExerCom; calculating exergies in Aspen (PC-version) user manual, Stork Comprimo report 61285-00-37-302-01
9. Liljedahl GN (2001) Technical and economic feasibility of CO_2 capture on an existing US coal-fired power plant. In: Proceedings of JPGC'01 2001 international joint power generation conference, June 2001, New Orleans. Paper no. JPGC2001/FACT-19174
10. Martínez I (2011) Exergy. http://webserver.dmt.upm.es/isidoro/. Accessed 5 July 2012
11. Querol E, Gonzalez-Regueral B, Perez-Benedito JL (2011) Novel application for exergy and thermoeconomic analysis of processes simulated with Aspen Plus®. Energy 36:964–974
12. Rivero R, Garfias M (2006) Standard chemical exergy of elements updated. Energy 31:3310–3326

13. Szagurt J (1988) Exergy analysis of thermal, chemical and metallurgical processes. Hemisphere Publishing Corporation, New York
14. Szargut J (1989) Chemical exergies of the elements. Appl Energy 32:269–286
15. Szargut J, Morris DR, Steward FR (1998) Exergy analysis of thermal, chemical, and metallurgical processes. Hemisphere Publishing Corporation, New York
16. Tsatsaronis G (1997) Exergy-aided cost minimization. Energy Convers Manag 38(15–17): 1535–1542
17. Valero A (2006) Exergy accounting: capabilities and drawbacks. Energy 31:164–180
18. Van Lier JJC, Woudstra N (2005) Thermodynamics for energy systems. Delft University Press, Delft
19. Zamfirescu C, Dincer I (2009) How much exergy one can obtain from incident solar radiation. J Appl Phys 105:044991-1–044991-5

Chapter 3
Matrix Algebra and Balances

Abstract For the mathematical representation of a process and for the achievement of mass, energy and exergy balances of the system, the incidence matrix is described and determined, for the subsystem of a process, piece of equipment by piece of equipment and for the two subsystems. It has also being defined and determined for the process as a whole, with the aim to establish the advantages and disadvantages of using a certain aggregation level, in addition to the equivalence between using a higher or lower one. In each case the mass, energy and exergy balances have been calculated, discussing the results obtained. As a final step, final thoughts over the advisability of using different levels of aggregation and the quality of the data which would be obtained are presented.

3.1 Introduction

Systems subjected to thermodynamic analyses can be considered as sets of elements (pieces of equipment or components) connected to each other and the environment through streams that exchange material and energy. As they can be rather complex, it is advisable to have the following resources:

- Simple and clear symbols for general formulations.
- Adequate representation for the automatic execution of calculations.

Graph theory and lineal algebra provide the necessary elements:

- Algebraic representation of the system structure through the incidence matrix.
- Vector representation of the material and energy flows.
- Bringing about the balances using matrix algebra.

This strategy greatly facilitates the formal approach to the problems and the calculations can be repeated time and time again, as usually needed for system analysis and synthesis. In this chapter these resources will be applied for the formulation and implementation of thermodynamic balances, always *in a steady state*.

E. Querol et al., *Practical Approach to Exergy and Thermoeconomic Analyses of Industrial Processes*, SpringerBriefs in Energy,
DOI: 10.1007/978-1-4471-4622-3_3, © The Author(s) 2013

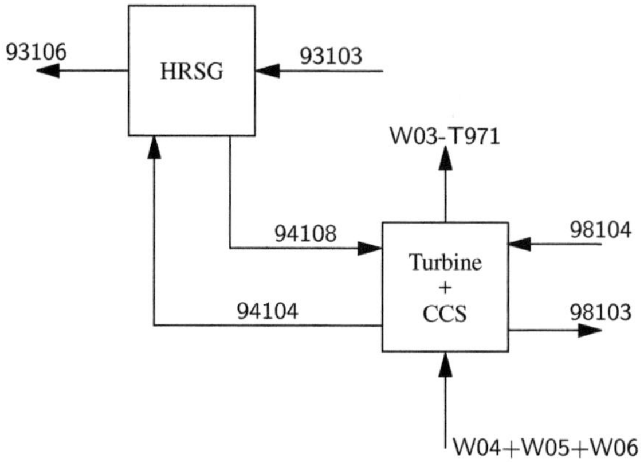

Fig. 3.1 Subsystems and associated streams

To simplify matters, the system under analysis (Figs. 1.2 and 1.3) will be reorganized into two subsystems possessing clear physical identities. Figure 3.1 shows the two subsystems with the various ingoing and outgoing streams:

3.2 Incidence Matrix: Physical Representation

The incidence matrix represents the physical reality of a system. It must be completed considering all the streams identified in the process: matter streams, work streams and heat streams [1]. We will apply this resource to study the heat recovery subsystem consisting of three pieces of equipment: E914, E915, E916, which are the major components of the boiler.

In this subsystem, $NH_3 + H_2O$ enters through one side as a liquid mixture (stream 94104) which is preheated in the economizer E916. At the exit, once heated, this stream (94105) is introduced into the boiler E915. Once in the vapour phase (stream 94106) is introduced in a superheater (E914). Stream 94106, once overheated (stream 94107), is expanded (stream 94108) in the T971 turbine generating power (W09-T971).

In the heat recovery subsystem, exhaust gases from the gas turbine (stream 93103) enter in counterflow. They first come into the heater, then the boiler (stream 93104) and later in the economizer (stream 63105). After being cooled, they are released into the atmosphere (stream 93106).

For the mathematical representation of any system and in particular this heat recovery subsystem, the following values will be assigned to the elements of the incidence matrix:

- $+1$ for streams entering a piece of equipment.
- -1 for streams leaving a piece of equipment.
- 0 if the stream does not affect a piece of equipment.

Table 3.1 Incidence matrix of the recovery boiler subsystem (minimum aggregation level)

Equipment	Streams							
	93103	93104	93105	93106	94104	94105	94106	94107
E914	1	−1	0	0	0	0	1	−1
E915	0	1	−1	0	0	1	−1	0
E916	0	0	1	−1	1	−1	0	0

Table 3.2 Incidence matrix of the recovery boiler subsystem (maximum aggregation level)

Equipment	Streams							
	93103	93104	93105	93106	94104	94105	94106	94107
HRSG	1	0	0	−1	1	0	0	−1

Furthermore, the matrix will have as many rows as pieces of equipment the system has, in this case 3 (E914, E915, E916) and as many columns as streams, thus 8:

- Four streams for the fumes: 93103, 93104, 93105, 93106.
- Five $NH_3 + H_2O$ mixture streams: 94104, 94105, 94106, 94107.

In this case, the incidence matrix $A_{(3\times 8)}$ results are shown in Table 3.1.

With this kind of representation, the incidence matrix of the same system or subsystem can be easily obtained with a higher aggregation level (i.e. considering the heat recovery subsystem as a whole). In case of using a higher aggregation level rows must be added, having as many rows as pieces of equipment appear in the new aggregation level. In this case, and for the heat recovery subsystem, it can be represented as a whole and therefore, with only one row. Changing the level of aggregation does not change the signs criterion, being the same for incoming and outgoing streams. When the level of aggregation changes and a higher one is used, streams inside the "new" represented subsystem disappear, as pieces of equipment do, and therefore they are not represented in the incidence matrix (Table 3.2).

Therefore, a lower level of aggregation will give more detail about the system. If a higher level of aggregation is adopted, results must be equivalent, but with less information about the system. Therefore, the choice of the level of aggregation used for the analysis of a system depends on the degree of detail required.

Extending this physical representation of the system as a whole and considering the level of aggregation that divides the system into two subsystems, Table 3.3 shows the incidence matrices of each subsystem and the full system's one at the highest state of aggregation.

As it can be concluded, the incidence matrix only gives information about the physical reality of the system and no information about its economic purpose is given.

Table 3.3 Incidence matrix of the complete system with aggregation level of two subsystems

Equipment	Streams									
	93103	93106	93104	93107	98103	98104	W03-T971	W04-P922	W05-P921	W06-P981
HRSG	1	−1	1	−1	0	0	0	0	0	0
Turbine + CCS	0	0	−1	1	−1	1	−1	1	1	1
System	1	−1	0	0	−1	1	−1	1	1	1

For the case under study, the incidence matrix is located in the range `B2:AH18` from sheet `A` of the workbook `WB1011`. The names of the streams and the pieces of equipment have been added to the columns (streams) and rows (pieces of equipment) to facilitate the reading of the sheet. The order of the streams is: matter streams (columns `B` to `AD`), work streams (columns `AE` to `AH`), and heat streams (none, as in this case there is no heat stream identified in the process). The elements of the incidence matrix have been automatically filled comparing the stream name, the piece of equipment name, with the information of the `BCorrM` rows 2 and 3, where it is indicated for each stream (matter, work, heat), the piece of equipment it comes from or it goes to.

3.3 Energy and Material Balances

By applying the principle of mass conservation, in steady state the mass entering and exiting a system is the same:

$$\sum \dot{m}_{\text{input}} = \sum \dot{m}_{\text{output}} \tag{3.1}$$

For m pieces of equipment connected by n streams, the m material balances can be written as:

$$A_{(m \times n)} \cdot M_{(n \times 1)} = 0_{(m \times 1)} \tag{3.2}$$

Due to the energy conservation principle, also the incoming energy must be equal to the outgoing energy as (3.3) shows:

$$\sum \dot{H}_{\text{input}} = \sum \dot{H}_{\text{output}} \tag{3.3}$$

Or in general, a system consisting of m pieces of equipment, connected by n streams, will verify the energy balance of all the pieces of equipment (3.4):

Table 3.4 Vectors with minimal mass and energy level of aggregation recovery boiler subsystem

Vectors	Streams			
	93103	93104	93105	93106
$\dot{m}$	42.08	42.08	42.08	42.08
$\dot{H}$	−14 708.52	−17 453.61	−27 968.07	−33 427.69
$\dot{B}$	11 818.08	10 172.95	4 923.25	3 304.75
Vectors	Streams			
	94104	94105	94106	94107
$\dot{m}$	8.20	8.20	8.20	8.20
$\dot{H}$	−71 603.20	−66 143.57	−55 629.11	−52 884.02
$\dot{B}$	99 974.82	101 317.47	105 519.36	106 834.25

Table 3.5 Material and energy balances of recovery boiler subsystem machine

Units	$\dot{m}$	$\dot{H}$
E914	0.00	0.00
E915	0.00	0.00
E916	0.00	−0.01

$$A_{(m\times n)} \cdot H_{(n\times 1)} = 0_{(m\times 1)} \tag{3.4}$$

Both Eqs. 3.2 and 3.3 make use of the same incidence matrix, the vector used being the only difference. This simplifies the balance calculations, with only the need of maintaining the same order, and considering that the non-material streams have a mass of 0 kg s^{-1}.

Once the incidence matrix of the system has been built, it would suffice to know the mass and energy vector for formulating the mass and energy balances of the system, simply by multiplying them by the incidence matrix. For the construction of these vectors and matrices, the information must be aggregated in the way in which matrices and vectors can be multiplied considering their dimensions.

In the following pages, the basic results and building of incidence matrices for different aggregation levels of the proposed facility will be shown. Detailed results for all the equipment and currents of the facility proposed can be found in the WB1001. As the reader comes along these tables and results, their main components, meaning and how they are obtained is explained.

In the case of the heat recovery subsystem at the lowest level of aggregation, mass and energy vectors are shown in Table 3.4. In this table, the first row shows, transposed, the mass vector, the second one the energy vector, and the third one the exergy vector:

The matter and energy balance of each of the pieces of equipment included in the subsystem are shown in Table 3.5.

If the system of Table 3.5 is considered as a whole, the mass and energy vectors are as shown in Table 3.6.

Table 3.7 shows the mass and energy balance of each of the identified subsystems (Fig. 3.1).

Table 3.6 Mass and energetic vector of the complete system

Vectors	Streams				
	93103	93106	94104	94107	98103
$\dot{m}$	42.08	42.08	8.20	8.20	200.00
$\dot{H}$	−14 708.52	−33 427.69	−71 603.20	−52 884.02	−3 172 700.00
Vectors	Streams				
	98104	W03-T971	W04-P922	W05-P921	W06-P981
$\dot{m}$	200.00	0.00	0.00	0.00	0.00
$\dot{H}$	−3 187 900.00	3 828.05	212.00	33.81	55.42

Table 3.7 Mass and energy balance of the whole system divided into two subsystems

Subsystems & System	$\dot{m}$	$\dot{H}$
HRSG	0.00	−0.01
Turbine + CCS	0.00	−7.64
System	0.00	−7.65

Tables 3.4 and 3.5 show that the expected values match the obtained ones for the mass balance, whereas in the case of the energy balance deviations from the expected theoretical results can be seen. In the analysis where the lowest level of aggregation is applied to the heat recovery subsystem (Table 3.5), in E915 and E916 some very small differences appear, while in the case of the complete system (Table 3.7) the differences are significant, if compared to the null values expected in theory.

Such differences may be due to the precision of operations, number of decimal places used or data used to estimate the thermodynamic properties of the streams. These differences can also be due to the precision of the measurement instruments at the facility. In addition, Aspen Plus® performs the energy balances until the result of the iterations is below a given tolerance in two consecutive steps. This complies with the convergence tolerance required, but as it is not fully balanced it can lead to errors in the calculations. In all cases, results must be compared with the incoming and outcoming energies (and matter flows), to analyse if a stream has not been considered in the analysis.

The balance calculations are easy to do in the `workbook WB1011`:

- The incidence matrix has been explained in Sect. 3.2.
- The vectors used are contained in the `MHBT sheet`. The mass vector occupies the range `B6AH6`, being the `AE6:AH6` filled with 0 (work streams), and the energy vector occupies the range `B7:AH7`.
- The calculations, and results, are written in the `Eq sheet, ranges B2:B18` (mass balance), and `C2:C18` (energy balance). The results' units are the units used in the vectors.

An additional energy balance (range `D2:D18` of `Eq sheet`) has been realized considering $H - H_0 + HHV$ (range `B8:AH8` of `MHBT sheet`), instead of the Aspen Plus® enthalpy values.

This is realized for comparison purposes and if a Sankey diagram is needed. This diagram shows a picture of the energy flows in arrows entering and exiting the system with a height proportional to the energy quantities.

3.4 Exergy Balance

Now that we have the algebraic resources for the formulation and implementation of the balances, it is very easy to deal with exergy. The exergy balance in steady state is represented by Eq. 3.5:

$$\sum \dot{B}_i = \dot{B}_{d,i} \tag{3.5}$$

$\dot{B}_{d,i}$ represents the destroyed exergy per unit time by each piece of equipment or subsystem. In general, for a system consisting of m pieces of equipment connected by n streams, the exergy balance will be expressed by Eq. 3.6.

$$A_{(m \times n)} \cdot B_{(n \times 1)} = B_{d,(m \times 1)} \tag{3.6}$$

This balance has the same form as the energy one, but there are some essential differences between them. The energy balance expresses a system of m equations that must fulfill the energy flows in order to satisfy the *First Law of Thermodynamics*. The exergy balance, determines the exergy destruction in each of the m pieces of equipment, as a result of the *Second Law of Thermodynamics*.

In the case of the heat recovery subsystem at the lowest level of aggregation, the exergy vector (Table 3.10) can be expressed, transposed, as in Table 3.8. The exergy balance per piece of equipment is shown in Table 3.9.

Table 3.8 Exergy vector recovery boiler subsystem

	Streams			
Vector	93103	93104	94105	94106
$\dot{B}$	11 818.08	10 172.95	4 923.25	3 304.75
	Streams			
Vector	94104	94105	94106	94107
$\dot{B}$	99 974.82	101 317.47	105 519.36	106 834.25

Table 3.9 Exergy balance: heat boiler subsystem (lowest and highest aggregation levels)

Units	$\dot{B}_{d,i}$
E914	330.24
E915	1 047.81
E916	275.85
HRSG	1 653.90

The complete system with the chosen aggregation level has the exergy vector shown in Table 3.10.

The exergy balance of the entire system is shown in Table 3.11.

In the case of exergy balances, as they give the exergy destroyed, it is impossible to establish with certainty whether the values are correct or not, so it is essential to make correct calculations, and to check the data, to detect possible errors of calculation or in the input data. Special care should be taken when the data is obtained from the Aspen Plus® simulations and other sources, as different precisions in these data may be used [2, 3].

The result of the exergy balance is the vector $B_{d(m\times 1)}$, called the *diagnostic vector* and represents the exergy that is destroyed in the pieces of equipment that make up the system. As exergy is an extensive property, the total destruction in the system is the sum of the irreversibility of each piece of equipment.

$$\dot{B}_d = \sum_{i=1}^{i=m} \dot{B}_{d,i} \tag{3.7}$$

Each $\dot{B}_{d,i}$ element of diagnostic vector $B_{d(m\times 1)}$ represents the exergy destroyed in a generic piece of equipment i and, therefore, the theoretically possible maximum energy saved in it. In (Eq. 3.7), $\dot{B}_d$ reflects the total exergy destroyed, or the total theoretical thermodynamic saving. The comparison of each $\dot{B}_{d,i}$ to the total $\dot{B}_d$ gives an idea of the relative weight of each piece of equipment in the destruction of exergy or *total plant irreversibility* by the *relative exergy destruction d_i factor*, defined by as follows:

$$d_i \equiv \frac{\dot{B}_{d,i}}{\dot{B}_d} \tag{3.8}$$

Table 3.10 Complete heat boiler subsystem exergy vector

Unit	Streams				
	93103	93106	94104	94107	98103
$\dot{B}$	11 818.08	3 304.75	99 974.82	106 834.25	35 370.51
Unit	Streams				
	98104	W03-T971	W04-P922	W05-P921	W06-P981
$\dot{B}$	34 722.93	3 828.05	212.00	33.81	55.42

Table 3.11 Exergy balance and relative exergy destruction of the two subsystems, and exergy balance of the whole system

Subsystems & system	$\dot{B}_{\mathrm{d},i}$	d_i [%]
HRSG	1 653.90	38
Turbine + CCS	2 685.03	62
System	4 338.93	100

Table 3.12 Exergy destroyed and relative exergy destruction in the recovery boiler subsystem

Unit	$\dot{B}_{d,i}$	d_i [%]
E914	330.24	20
E915	1 047.81	63
E916	275.85	17
HRSG	1 653.90	100

In the case of the heat recovery subsystem at the lowest level of aggregation, the rate of destruction or contribution of each piece of equipment to the total exergy destruction of the subsystem is shown in Table 3.12.

This table shows that the evaporator E915 is the piece of equipment in which more exergy is destroyed owing to the greater average temperature difference between warm and cold streams. In the case of the economizer and superheater, the differences are very similar and exergy destruction ratios as well. For the complete system, the contribution of each subsystem to the irreversibility of the process is shown in Table 3.11.

In the exergy balance, it is shown that the subsystem that destroys more exergy is the turbine and condensation subsystem. Exergy destruction caused by this subsystem represents 61 % of the global amount of energy destroyed. This subsystem destroys twice as much as the heat recovery subsystem; mainly owing to its aim. The main function of a condensation system is to destroy exergy.

For the whole case, and following with the `WB1011 workbook`, the Exergy vector is available in `MHBT!B9:AH9` (this means `range B9:AH9` from the `MHBT sheet`, according to Microsoft Excel® nomenclature), and the diagnostic vector has been calculated in `Eq!E2:E18`. Additionally in the same `workbook WB1011`, the relative destruction vector has been calculated for the whole system in `Eq!F2:F18` under the name `dr`.

3.5 Conclusions

The analysis of a plant or facility may be performed in principle with all the detail desired, reaching each piece of equipment or even splitting some down into several elements. The lower the aggregation level, the higher the incidence matrix complexity. If pieces of equipment are grouped into subsets of the system, the aggregation level increases and the incidence matrix simplifies. The rows of this matrix corresponding to elements that are grouped in a subset will be replaced by a single one, a sum of them, which represents the subset. The more detailed the analysis, with a therefore lower level of aggregation, the greater the chances of a thorough analysis and investigation of the results obtained. This will make it possible to check for more possible improvements. In each particular case, the aggregation level will be low enough so as to achieve the objectives of the analysis, with the least possible complexity.

References

1. Bram S (1997) Exergy analysis tools for Aspen applied to evaporative cycle design. Energy Convers Manag 38(15–17):1613–1624
2. Hiendrink AP (1996) Exergy analysis with a flowsheeting simulator. I. Theory; calculating exergies of material streams. Chem Eng Sci 51(20):4693–4700
3. Hiendrink AP (1996) Exergy analysis with a flowsheeting simulator. II. Application; synthesis gas production from natural gas. Chem Eng Sci 51(20):4701–4715

Chapter 4
Exergetic Cost

Abstract This chapter addresses the representation of any system based on its resources, products and wastes (*R/P/I representation*). This will identify the resources needed to generate the products, and will provide a thorough basis for performance evaluation. The same basis will be used to establish the concept of *exergetic cost* of a stream, measured by the exergy required to produce it. The standpoint will be economic, but handling exergy instead of monetary amounts. The concept of branching will be established for the cases in which there is more than one output from a piece of equipment, introducing the *augmented matrix* for the formulation of the exergetic cost balance. Performance evaluation concepts will be rationally defined, thus easing the analysis of industrial processes and setting the unit exergetic cost concept.

4.1 Introduction

The application of economic concepts and judgments (utility of each stream in the system) must be applied when doing an exergetic analysis of a facility. In addition to the physical structure of the system, its *economic* or productive structure must be known. A stream can be characterized as a *resource* consumed by a piece of equipment or a *product* generated by it [4]. There is also the need to identify the outputs of a system that do not have any economic value or that may even be harmful, which will be classified as waste. It is important to recognize that while the physical structure of a system is unique, its economic structure depends on the use or its intended application. With the same physical structure, there can be several potential economic alternatives, which will lead to different results. In addition, the evaluation of the efficiency or performance of a piece of equipment will be based on economic criteria, and not only in its thermodynamic perfection.

E. Querol et al., *Practical Approach to Exergy and Thermoeconomic Analyses of Industrial Processes*, SpringerBriefs in Energy,
DOI: 10.1007/978-1-4471-4622-3_4, © The Author(s) 2013

4.2 "R/P/I" Representation

According to the *economic structure* of the system, the incoming or outgoing currents in each piece of equipment can be classified as a *resource*, *product* or *waste* [3, 14]. Product P of an item represents the desired useful effect it provides, according to its purpose. Resource R represents the resource consumed to generate the product [2, 8, 10]. R and P may include more than one incoming or outgoing current. An equipment can have *waste* or *loss* outflows to the *environment* (with or without flow of matter), with no useful effect; they are put together as *waste* I of the unit. As result of this classification, all equipment, regardless of its complexity, may be represented in the compact form drawn in Fig. 4.1, with R, P and I expressed in terms of exergetic flow. It must be noted that the *R/P/I representation* requires prior identification of resources, products and wastes, by *economic* value judgments, beyond the physical structure of the system.

To illustrate how to proceed, Fig. 4.2 outlines some typical cases. Case (a) corresponds to a turbine, whose mission is to produce mechanical work from the exergy transferred by a fluid; the resource is, therefore, the exergy drop $\dot{B}_1 - \dot{B}_2$ of the fluid and the product will be the useful work $\dot{B}_3$ done by the piece of equipment or system. In those situations, where the turbine operate under free escape to the atmosphere, $\dot{B}_2$ would be the waste and $\dot{B}_1$ the resource. In case (b), the compressor has the inverse mission, to increase the exergy of a fluid through the use of work; the $\dot{B}_2 - \dot{B}_1$ increase is now the product and the flow of incoming work $\dot{B}_3$ the resource. The question is clear to the combustion chamber of case (c): the resource is the sum $\dot{B}_1 + \dot{B}_2$ of the exergy flows of fuel and oxidizer, while the product is the exergy $\dot{B}_3$ of the combustion gases. Finally, case (d), the purpose of a steam boiler is to increase the exergy of the feed water thanks to the support of combustion. As in a combustion chamber, the resource is the sum $\dot{B}_1 + \dot{B}_2$ of the exergy flows of fuel and oxidizer. The product will be the difference $\dot{B}_6 - \dot{B}_5$ between the exergy flows of live steam and feed water. Assuming that the combustion gases and ash are ejected into the *environment* after passing through all the energy recovery devices, which are considered included in the boiler, they will have the character of waste; exergy flow $\dot{I}$ will be $\dot{B}_3 + \dot{B}_4$. The examples in Fig. 4.2 show that the resource and the product of a device may include both inbound and outbound flows interchangeably [3].

The RPI classification must be done for all the streams in each piece of equipment of the system. A stream can therefore have different classifications depending on the equipment unit although it is convenient that the RPI of a stream entering or exiting the system is the same both for the equipment unit and for the system as a whole.

This happens with the case under analysis (see Doc2003), where the general rules given in Fig. 4.2 have not been followed in stream `98104`, which is classified as a resource, because it is a resource of the whole system, so it has been also classified as a resource for pump `P981`, although initially will be classified as a product due to the exergy increase in the fluid produced in the pump by the work consumed by it.

Figure 4.3 outlines the case of a general equipment E, whose inputs and outputs have been identified as resources, products or wastes.

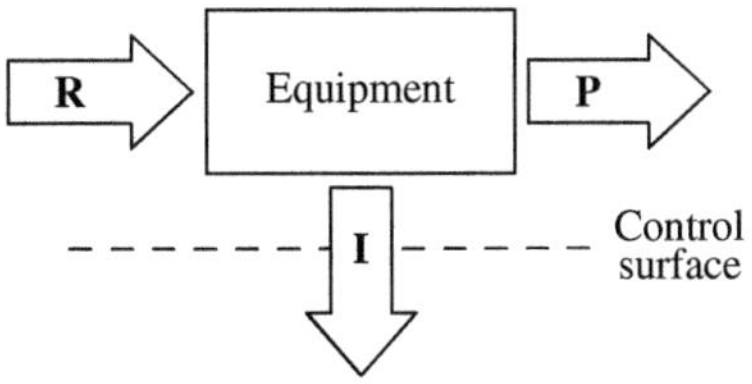

Fig. 4.1 R/P/I classification of a piece of equipment

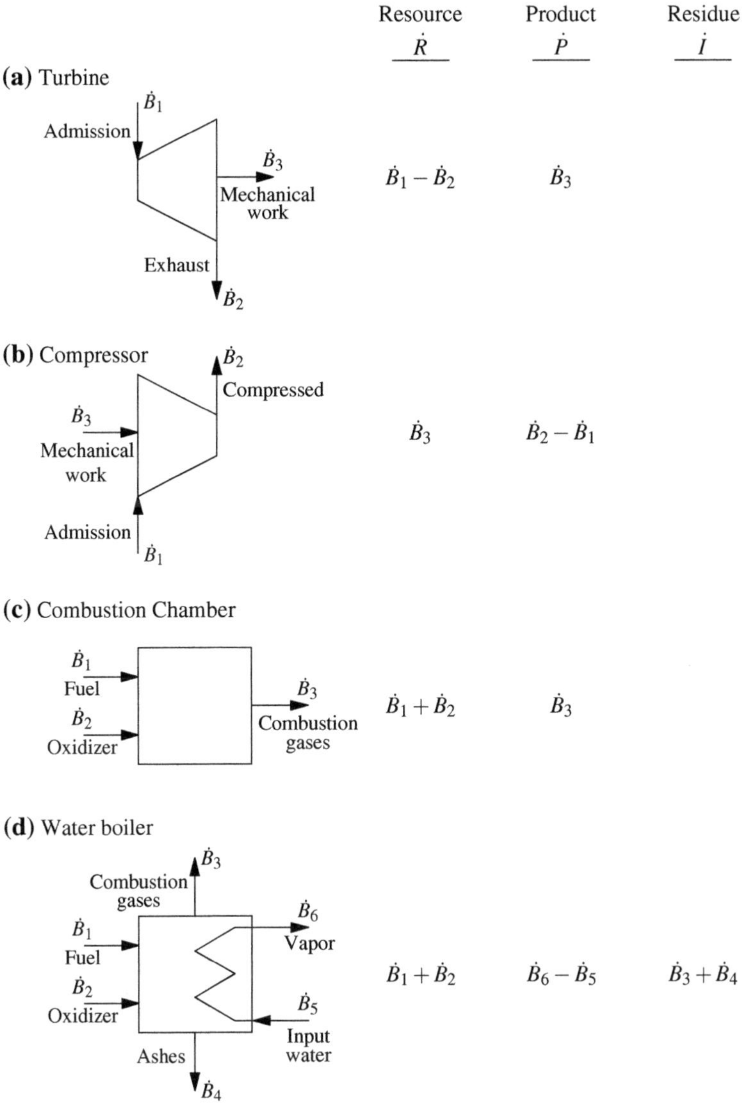

Fig. 4.2 Common "R/P/I" classification for typical equipment

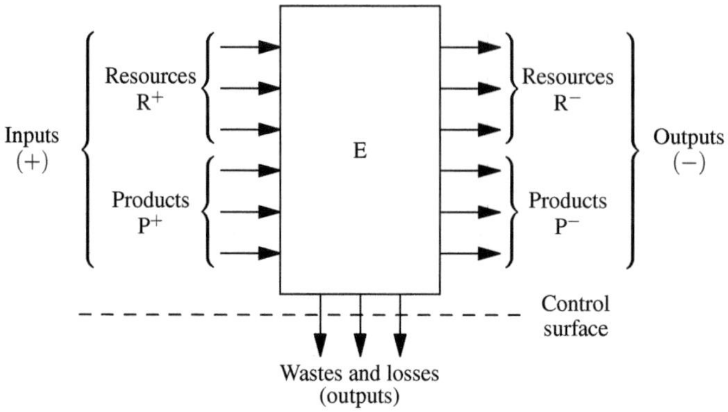

Fig. 4.3 General case for a piece of equipment *E*

In general, for open systems, the *control surface* is the geometrical surface that separates the system from the environment, being the part of the opened system contained inside of the control surface the control volume. For a closed system, were a fixed mass is contained inside a control surface, this fixed quantity is called *control mass*.

The resource of an item is defined as the addition of exergy flows classified as incoming resources minus the sum of the outgoing ones of the same class, as shown in Eq. 4.1. The superscripts + and − respectively identify ingoing and outgoing flows, as the former provide exergy and the latter subtract it:

$$\dot{R} \equiv \sum \dot{B}_R^+ - \sum \dot{B}_R^- \tag{4.1}$$

Product $\dot{P}$ is defined as the sum of outgoing exergetic flows classified as products minus the sum of the ingoing ones of the same class, Eq. 4.2 since the first involves power outputs and the latter, inputs:

$$\dot{P} \equiv \sum \dot{B}_P^- - \sum \dot{B}_P^+ \tag{4.2}$$

Regarding $\dot{I}$, it is broadly defined as the sum of all outflows to the environment, (Eq. 4.3) that are characterized as waste or loss (with or without matter flow), without any useful result or effect:

$$\dot{I} \equiv \sum \dot{B}_I \tag{4.3}$$

If the product (4.2) and the waste (4.3) are subtracted from the resource (4.1), it results in (4.4) and (4.5), which is the exergy balance of the equipment considered in *R/P/I representation*.

Table 4.1 R/P/I classification of each process subsystem

Equipment/stream	R	P	I
HRSG	93103	94107-94104	93106
Turbine + CCS	W04+W05+W06+98104+94107	94104+W03	98103

$$\dot{R} - \dot{P} - \dot{I} = \left(\sum \dot{B}_R^+ + \sum \dot{B}_P^+\right) - \left(\dot{B}_R^- + \dot{B}_P^- + \dot{B}_I^-\right)$$
$$= \sum \dot{B}^+ - \sum \dot{B}^- = \dot{B}_d \quad (4.4)$$
$$\dot{R} = \dot{P} + \dot{I} + \dot{B}_d \quad (4.5)$$

As can be seen, *R* and *P* can be simultaneously inputs and outputs of each considered unit. However, the sign criteria considered is consistent with the intuition: each piece of equipment must consume (input) a resource and its purpose is to produce (output) a valuable product as well as an unavoidable waste (output), which is the logic that underpins Eq. 4.5 and Fig. 4.1.

Some authors do not consider the waste term $\dot{I}$, and thus its value increases the exergy destruction, as already said. They also name the resource as fuel, and therefore instead of *RPI*, they use the *FP* representation. In this book the term resource will be used instead of fuel, because *fuel* seems to be constrained only for power generation, while *resource* is more general and therefore applicable to more systems [3].

In the analyzed process there will be a classification of incoming and outgoing flows of each of the subsystems in order to determine its economic structure. Table 4.1 shows the R/P/I classification of each of the subsystems.

By going into detail on each of the subsystems that form the generation system, the R/P/I structure chosen in each case will be analyzed.

- *HRSG subsystem*: In this case, the exhaust gases leaving the gas turbine already existing in the compression station are considered as the only resource, because they are used to heat the liquid fluid from the condensation system. Once cooled in the boiler, the output exhaust gases, having yielded most of their exergy, are considered waste of no economic value.
- *Turbine + CCS*: the product of this system is the electricity generated by the steam turbine, and the high pressure work fluid stream 94104, being the resources the electricity needed to move the pumps, the environmental water used in the condensation part of the subsystem and the exergy of the incoming stream 94107. This exergy is first used in the turbine to generate electricity and later is destroyed in the condensation subsystem.

To symbolize the exposed R/P/I representation in matrix form the following matrices will be defined:

(a) *Resource Matrix* A_R. To each element $a_{R,ij}$, one of the following values is assigned:

- $+1$, if current j is a resource entering unit i.
- -1, if current j is a resource exiting unit i.
- 0, if current j is not a resource of unit i.

(b) *Product Matrix* A_P. To its element $a_{P,ij}$, one of the following values is assigned:

- $+1$, if current j is a product exiting unit i.
- -1, if current j is a product entering unit i.
- 0, if current j is not a product of unit i.

(c) *Waste Matrix* A_I. To its element $a_{I,ij}$, one of the following values is assigned:

- $+1$, if current j is a residue/loss of unit i (it is always an output).
- 0, if current j is not a residue/loss of unit i.

These three matrices are respectively the `R`, `P` and `I sheets` from the case `workbook WB1011`.

The (a) sign criteria agrees with the incidence matrix of Sect. 3.2. The (b) and (c) ones are opposed. As all the currents of each unit have to be classified as R, P or I and only one of them, Eq. 4.6 must be verified, where the incidence matrix can be constructed with the three matrices:

$$A_{(m\times n)} = A_{R,(m\times n)} - A_{P,(m\times n)} - A_{I,(m\times n)} \tag{4.6}$$

If the resource, product and waste vectors are defined (Eq. 4.7), as the exergy of each of the streams classified as resource, product, and waste [8], then the Eq. 4.8 must be verified, which determines said vectors.

$$R_{(m\times 1)} \equiv \begin{bmatrix} \dot{R}_1 \\ \vdots \\ \dot{R}_m \end{bmatrix} \quad ; \quad P_{(m\times 1)} \equiv \begin{bmatrix} \dot{P}_1 \\ \vdots \\ \dot{P}_m \end{bmatrix} \quad ; \quad I_{(m\times 1)} \equiv \begin{bmatrix} \dot{I}_1 \\ \vdots \\ \dot{I}_m \end{bmatrix} \tag{4.7}$$

$$\left.\begin{array}{r} A_{R,(m\times n)} \cdot B_{(n\times 1)} = R_{(m\times 1)} \\ A_{P,(m\times n)} \cdot B_{(n\times 1)} = P_{(m\times 1)} \\ A_{I,(m\times n)} \cdot B_{(n\times 1)} = I_{(m\times 1)} \end{array}\right\} \tag{4.8}$$

As each equipment unit i has to satisfy (4.9), this relationship can be written in vector form (4.10), which is the matrix expression of the exergy balance in the R/P/I form.

$$\dot{R}_i - \dot{P}_i - \dot{I}_i = \dot{B}_{d,i} \tag{4.9}$$

$$R_{(m\times 1)} - P_{(m\times 1)} - I_{(m\times 1)} = B_{d,(m\times 1)} \tag{4.10}$$

In the case under analysis the $R_{(m\times 1)}$, $P_{(m\times 1)}$, $I_{(m\times 1)}$ vectors are present in the `WB1011` web material, `sheet Eq, columns G, H, I` respectively.

The application of (4.8) in (4.10) results in (4.11) and as a consequence of (4.6), this result becomes (4.12), which coincides with the conventional exergy balance, Eq. 3.6.

$$\left(A_{R,(m\times n)} - A_{P,(m\times n)} - A_{I,(m\times n)}\right) \cdot B_{(n\times 1)} = B_{d,(m\times 1)} \tag{4.11}$$

$$A_{(m\times n)} \cdot B_{(n\times 1)} = B_{d,(m\times 1)} \tag{4.12}$$

4.3 Exergetic Cost

Let us consider any system at maximum aggregation level. Its R/P/I representation will have the form drawn in Fig. 4.1. The exergetic cost P^* is defined as the required exergetic flow used to obtain it, which in this case is, of course, equal to $\dot{R}$, the exergetic value of the resource. If a piece of equipment is considered, its resource will have an exergetic cost R^* (resulting exergetic flow consumed for the generation of the resource in the system, which has to be calculated) [9, 14]. For any equipment unit, an exergetic cost balance will be verified according to (4.13), which represents that the exergetic cost of the product has to be equal to that of the resource, because the exergetic cost is a variable cost, so no fixed cost from the piece of equipment is considered:

$$R^* = P^* \tag{4.13}$$

When the resource comes from the environment (through the control surface of the system), its cost equals its exergy:

$$B_{in}^* \equiv \dot{B}_{in} \tag{4.14}$$

The exergy that was needed to produce it is an *external cost*, which does not affect the system under study, although it is possible also to assign an exergetic cost through a life cycle analysis.

According to the economic practice, the exergetic cost is collected entirely by the product (because it is the only saleable stream), resulting in a null waste cost (4.15):

$$I^* \equiv 0 \tag{4.15}$$

Equation 4.15 does not mean that the waste is not involved in the cost balance or that the cost of the waste is 0. What it really means is that the cost of the waste must be derived to the product, which is really the consequence of this equation.

The influence of waste production is high, as all the exergy of the resources exiting as waste is not exiting in the product flow, which means that less product is being obtained, and therefore the cost of the specific flow of the product is being increased (i.e. $\mathrm{kJ\,kg^{-1}}$, $\mathrm{kJ\,m^{-3}}$, $\mathrm{kJ\,kWh^{-1}}$ ...). With this concept, the exergetic cost of a waste or the exergy destroyed can be quantified as the unit exergetic cost of the resource multiplied by the exergy of the waste flow or of the exergy destroyed by the unit.

As R, P and I are groups of physical streams, the exergetic cost concept can also be applied to the latter. The exergetic cost B_j^* of a stream is defined as the exergy $\dot{B}$ consumed to produce the stream. The exergy of a stream is an objective thermodynamic property itself, determined by its state and composition. Its exergetic cost, however, will depend on the particular process used for its production. A stream defined by its temperature, pressure, vapour fraction, and composition will have different exergetic costs if different processes are used to create it, and thus according to the thermodynamic perfection of the process characterized by the quantity of the resources consumed in the generation of the stream.

To compare both magnitudes, the *unit exergetic cost* κ_j^* of a stream j is defined as the *exergy consumed* to obtain one unit of exergy of it. This unit cost includes the effect of thermodynamic perfection of the process and economic criteria applied for the determination of exergy costs:

$$\kappa_j^* \equiv \frac{B_j^*}{\dot{B}_j} \tag{4.16}$$

The formal expressions to calculate R^*, P^* and I^* are shown in (4.17). As it can be seen these equations are formally the same as (4.1), (4.2) and (4.3) where the exergy of a resource, product or waste was calculated:

$$\begin{aligned} R^* &\equiv \sum B_R^{*+} - \sum B_R^{*-} \\ P^* &\equiv \sum B_P^{*-} - \sum B_P^{*+} \\ I^* &\equiv \sum B_I^* \end{aligned} \tag{4.17}$$

The last condition needed to do an exergetic cost balance is (4.15) assigning a null exergetic cost to waste. This condition must be applied when needed to every unit to derive all costs to the product flow:

$$B_I^* \equiv 0 \tag{4.18}$$

As a consequence of Eq. 4.13, Eq. 4.19 is satisfied, expressing the *exergetic cost balance referring to the streams*. This balance indicates that the *exergetic cost of outgoing flows must be equal to that of the incoming ones*:

$$\sum B^{*+} = \sum B^{*-} \tag{4.19}$$

Therefore, the exergetic cost is conservative and formally settles balances identical to the energetic ones. For any system in general, an *exergetic cost balance* can be written as follows (4.20) with the *exergetic cost vector* instead of the *energy vector*:

$$A_{(m\times n)} \cdot B^*_{(n\times 1)} = 0_{(m\times 1)} \tag{4.20}$$

The exergetic cost balance (4.20) provides m equations (one per unit of equipment) to determine the n exergetic costs (one per stream). Generally, it is always $n > m$, [5]. This is due to the following two causes [2]:

- *System inputs*, crossing the control surface.
- *Branchings* (internal and external) in pieces of equipment with more than one output.

Owing to it, the exergetic cost balance (4.13) does not provide a sufficient number of equations to determine the exergetic costs. The additional equations must be based on economic considerations, beyond the field of thermodynamics, and refer to the inputs, wastes and branchings. The firsts provide as many equations as inputs to the system.

4.4 Branchings

Branchings can be internal or external, depending on whether they cross the control surface (the surface surrounding the system under analysis) or not.

4.4.1 Internal Branchings

Internal branchings occur in pieces of equipment with two or more outgoing streams, which in turn are inputs in other units in the system. Figure 4.4 outlines the situation.

The depicted piece of equipment has N outputs. Supposing that output 1 is a product, and that output s is also a product both streams have the same unit exergetic cost represented by (4.21), which implies that the cost to their generation is distributed among these streams according to their exergy [5]: the unit exergetic costs is the same for products of the same importance exiting the same piece of equipment.

$$\kappa_s^* = \kappa_1^* \tag{4.21}$$

$$\frac{B_s^*}{\dot{B}_s} = \frac{B_1^*}{\dot{B}_1} = \kappa_1^* \tag{4.22}$$

The economic rational for this approach is very reasonable: the exergetic cost is shared in proportion to the exergy of the outputs, which represent their respective

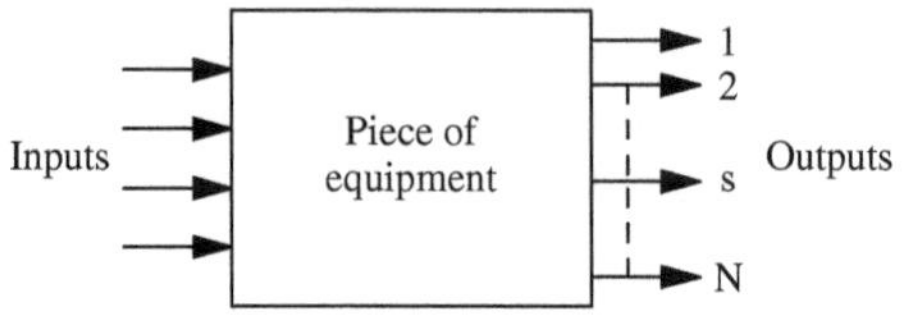

Fig. 4.4 Product output case

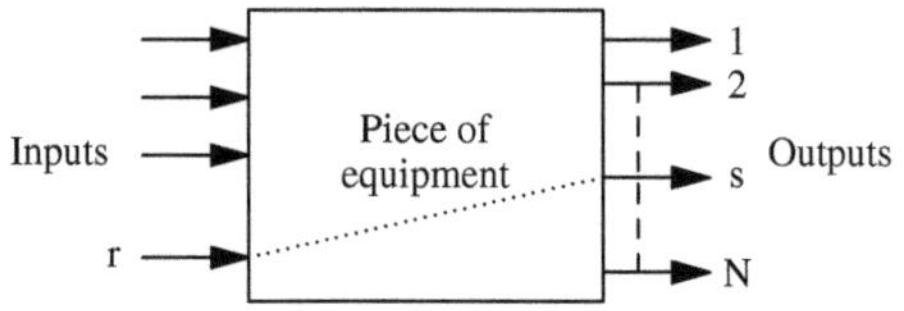

Fig. 4.5 Resource output case

useful energy flows. These results indicate that when the outputs are products, the exergy destruction is distributed between their exergetic costs in proportion to their respective exergies. This economic decision, where two exiting products of a piece of equipment share their unit exergetic cost, is known as the *P-principle* [5].

This happens with S921, in which an incoming stream is divided into two streams of different composition, but both useful: one is to enrich the NH_3 content of the new working fluid, and the other is used to dilute the NH_3 content of the used working fluid to condense it at a higher temperature.

In the case of a resource output, as in Fig. 4.5, the output s is a resource, associated with the resource input. Then the output resource stream has a unit exergetic cost equal to that of the input resource stream, as shown by (4.23) and (4.24):

$$\kappa_s^* = \kappa_r^* \tag{4.23}$$

$$\frac{B_s^*}{\dot{B}_s} = \frac{B_r^*}{\dot{B}_r} = \kappa_r^* \tag{4.24}$$

In this case, the unit exergetic cost of the resource is maintained, therefore for the input and output resource streams, their exergetic cost becomes proportional to their exergy. From (4.24), it can be concluded that the exergetic cost of the exergy transferred to the equipment is proportional to it, as shown by (4.25). This economic decision, where input and output resource streams of a piece of equipment share their unit exergetic cost, is known as the *F-Principle*, or *R-Principle* (*Resource* instead of *Fuel*).

$$\frac{B_r^* - B_s^*}{\dot{B}_r - \dot{B}_s} = \kappa_r^* \tag{4.25}$$

In this case, the exergetic cost of the resource output is not affected by the destruction of exergy.

Fig. 4.6 External branchings

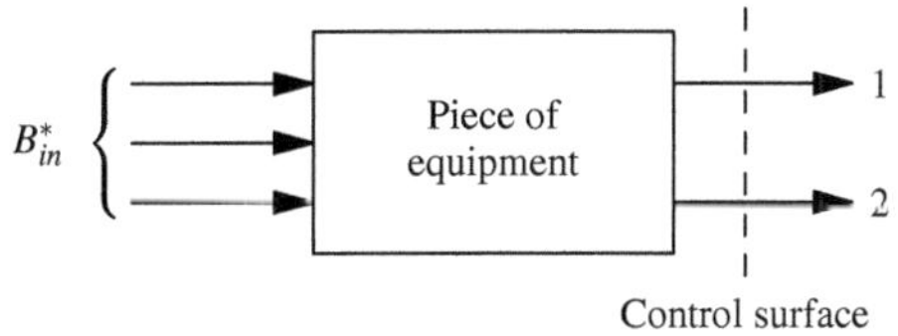

Therefore an equation like (4.24) or (4.25) will be added for each piece of equipment with branchings. For a total of N outputs, $N - 1$ additional equations will be available, which together with the exergetic cost balance (4.19) of each piece of equipment, supplies the N equations needed for calculating the exergetic costs of the outputs.

4.4.2 External Branchings

A system with two outputs, 1 and 2, will be considered, which are *system outputs*, i.e. crossing the control surface, as sketched in Fig. 4.6.

The total exergetic cost of the input will be represented by B^*_{in}. Its exergetic cost balance will be represented by (4.26), requiring an additional condition to determine the exergetic costs of the two outputs.

$$B^*_{in} = B^*_1 + B^*_2 \tag{4.26}$$

Depending on the nature of the outputs, there are three possible cases:

(a) *Two main products.* If there are no particular circumstances that demand specific treatment for each of the two outputs, and they are product outputs, the P-Principle (4.22) will be applied and the same unit exergetic cost is assigned to both outputs

$$\frac{B^*_1}{\dot{B}_1} = \frac{B^*_2}{\dot{B}_2} = \kappa^* \tag{4.27}$$

(b) *A by-product.* Now output 1 is the only main product and output 2 is a by-product. If there is no other condition of internal origin, an exergetic cost ω may be assigned to output 2 equal to the exergy consumed in the best available process to produce that stream.
This means that the by-product has an exergetic value ω, which is the minimum exergetic cost at which it could be produced.

$$B^*_2 \equiv \omega \tag{4.28}$$

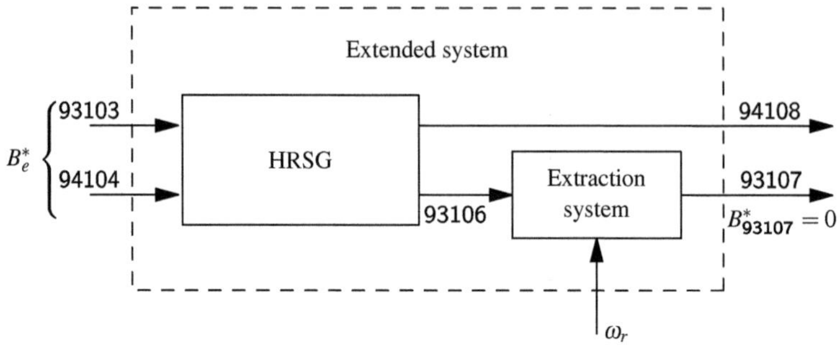

Fig. 4.7 Flue gases evacuation system and recovery boiler subsystem

In any case, (4.29) can be draw from the exergetic cost balance (4.26)

$$B_1^* = B_{in}^* - B_2^* = B_{in}^* - \omega \tag{4.29}$$

The higher the ω, the lower the exergetic cost B_1^* of the main product.

(c) *Waste*. If Output 2 is a waste, its exergetic cost is null (4.30), so (4.31) will be fulfilled and the exergetic cost B_{in}^* will be collected by Product 1.

$$B_2^* \equiv 0 \tag{4.30}$$

$$B_1^* = B_{in}^* \tag{4.31}$$

Sometimes an ancillary facility is required to remove or evacuate a waste (pump, fan, belt conveyor, etc.) [7]. Let us suppose that in the process under analysis, the HRSG subsystem requires a fan to evacuate the exhaust gases leading them to atmospheric pressure, as represented in Fig. 4.7. The fan is not considered a part of the HRSG subsystem though it is needed for it to work, consuming an amount of exergy ω_r with the best technology available. In the case under study, the outgoing stream of the fan ventilator is a new one (therefore not contained in the original HRSG subsystem) and is named 93107. The exergetic cost balance of the extraction equipment would be expressed by (4.32), where the exergetic cost of the waste (stream 93107) must be zero.

$$B^*_{93106} + \omega_r = B^*_{93107} = 0 \tag{4.32}$$

As the exergetic cost assigned to the waste is zero, the exergetic cost of the exhaust gases stream at the output of the boiler would be negative, and its value will be equal to the exergy consumed by the fan.

$$B^*_{93106} = -\omega_r \tag{4.33}$$

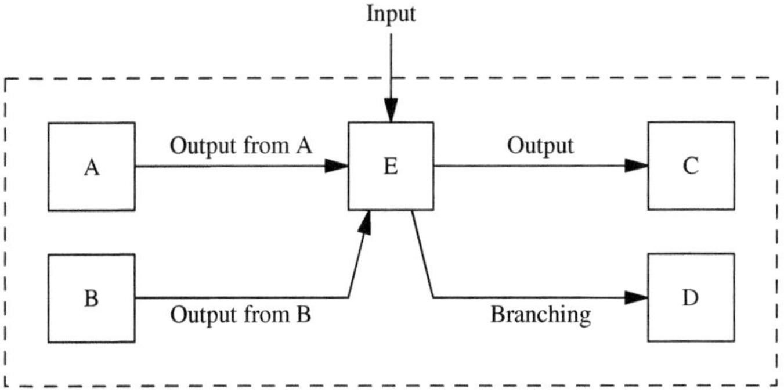

Fig. 4.8 Piece of equipment E with inputs, outputs and branchings

Therefore, the exergetic cost balance of the original recovery boiler subsystem in this case would be as follows.

$$B_{in}^{*} = B_{93104}^{*} + B_{93106}^{*} = B_{93107}^{*} - \omega_r \tag{4.34}$$

Therefore the exergetic cost balance of the extended system (extraction system and HRSG) will be the one shown in (4.35), equivalent to (4.34).

$$B_{in}^{*} + \omega_r = B_{93107}^{*} \tag{4.35}$$

Therefore, when joining the evacuation equipment (in this case, a fan) to the system, the cost of the waste ω_r disposal is added to the B_{in}^{*} of the inputs, as an additional one (4.35). On the other hand, if the evacuation equipment (in this case, a fan) is not part of the system but it must collect the cost of removal, a negative value must be assigned to the output waste of the system.

4.5 Determination of the Exergetic Costs

The exergetic cost of an incoming resource equals its exergy and the criteria for branchings can be obtained from Eqs. 4.22, 4.24, 4.28 and 4.30. These expressions provide the elements necessary for the determination of the exergetic costs of the inputs and branchings, providing the additional equations $n - m$ that, together with the m equations given by the exergetic cost balance (4.14), will make the exergetic cost calculation of the n streams of the system possible.

To do this, the existing general relationship between the total number n of streams, the m number of pieces of equipment, and the numbers b and i of branchings and inputs will be deduced [6]. Figure 4.8 shows a piece of equipment E, connected to the various possible types. In general, the following facts can be stated:

- Any equipment has at least one output.
- The total number of outputs minus one gives the number of branchings of the unit.

- Inputs from other units have already been computed as outputs or branchings of previous units.
- System inputs crossing the control surface must also be added to the computation of total streams.

So (4.36) is verified

$$n = m + i + b \tag{4.36}$$

This result indicates that if the m equations of system (4.20) express the exergetic cost balance, the additional $n - m = i + b$ equations provided by the inputs and branches will be added to obtain the n total number of equations required for calculating the n streams' exergetic costs [10].

Matrix treatment of the problem is simple. An $\alpha_{(n-m)\times n}$ matrix is defined, whose rows will have all elements zero, excluding the following ones:

- *Inputs*. Value 1 for each α_{ei} element, which corresponds to an input (column of stream i) to equipment unit e (row of unit of equipment e).
- *By-products*. Value 1 for each α_{eb} element relative to by-product b from equipment e.
- *Wastes*. Value 1 for each α_{el} element referring to waste l originated in equipment e.
- *Branchings*. Value $+1/\dot{B}_j$ in the column corresponding to stream j and value $-1/\dot{B}_k$ in the column corresponding to stream k.

This matrix, present on the `WB1011` (web content) `A!B19:AH34`, for our study case. Usually the most appropriate way to deal with the additional equations required is to go by with the following order:

- Add one Eq. 4.15 to each waste l exiting the system. Streams 93106, 98103 of the installation. (`rows 19,20` of the economic structure matrix `WB1011, sheet A`).
- Look the system as a whole and according to the RPI classification, add one Eq. 4.15 to each resource R entering the system. In the case under study this has been done for streams 93103, 98104 (`rows 21,24` of the economic structure matrix `WB1011, sheet A`).
- Add one Eq. 4.28 to each byproduct P exiting the system. No stream is, in this case, in the installation, analyzed.
- Make a list of the exits of each equipment, and consider one in it as much equations as streams minus one exiting the equipment, that have not been considered in the previous step. This has been done in `WB1011, sheet Eq, column L`. All the equations needed in this case will be like Eq. 4.27, using the R-Principle (F-Principle) or the P-Principle shown in Sect. 4.4.1 In the installation under study `rows 22,23, and 25-34 (WB1011, sheet A)`, correspond to equations like this.

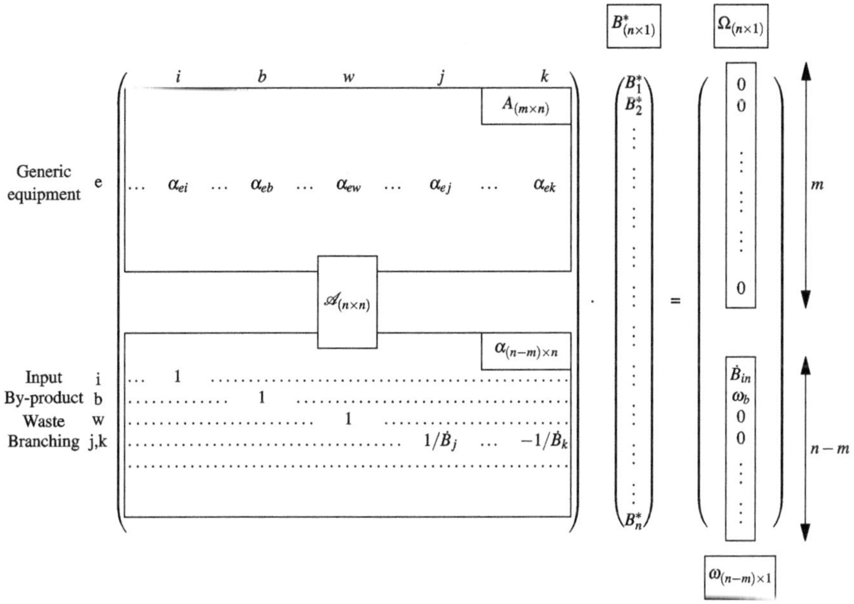

Fig. 4.9 Augmented matrix components

Matrix $\alpha_{(n-m)\times n}$ represents the *economic structure* of the system and therefore is called the *economy matrix*. On the other hand, the incidence matrix represents its *physical structure*, as seen in Sect. 3.2. A vector $\omega_{(n-m)\times l}$, called the *defined exergetic cost vector*, is also defined, whose elements have the following values:

- *Inputs*: $\dot{B}_{in}$
- *By-products*: ω_b
- *Wastes*: 0
- *Branchings*: 0

As shown in the bottom part of Fig. 4.9, the matrix product $\alpha_{(n-m)\times n} \cdot B^*_{(n\times l)}$, equal to $\omega_{(n-m)\times l}$, obviously leads to the additional required $n - m$ equations [12, 13]. At the top of the incidence matrix $\mathscr{A}$, products appear, by the exergy cost vector B^*, equalled to a zero vector of dimension m. This product expresses the exergy cost balance given by (4.20). It can be seen that matrices A and α may be combined in a single square matrix $\mathscr{A}$ of $(n \times n)$.

$$\mathscr{A} \equiv \begin{bmatrix} A \\ \cdots \\ \alpha \end{bmatrix} \tag{4.37}$$

This matrix is contained in the `A sheet` of `WB1011`, and has a dimension of 33 × 33, being 17 the pieces of equipment m of the installation and 33 the number of streams n, and therefore 16 additional equations have been used in the economy matrix $(n - m)$.

Additionally, the *assigned exergetic cost vector* Ω is defined, with dimensions $(n \times 1)$, whose first m elements are zero and the remaining $(n - m)$ are those of the defined exergetic cost ω:

$$\Omega \equiv \begin{bmatrix} 0 \\ \cdots \\ \omega \end{bmatrix} \tag{4.38}$$

This allows to write the exergetic cost balance (4.20) in the following compact form:

$$\mathscr{A}_{(n \times n)} \cdot B^*_{(n \times 1)} = \Omega_{(n \times 1)} \tag{4.39}$$

The square matrix $\mathscr{A}$, of dimension $n \times n$, the result of expanding the incidence matrix A with the economy matrix α, is called *augmented matrix* and vector Ω of $n \times 1$ dimensions, *assigned exergetic costs vector.*

Multiplying both terms of (4.39) by the matrix $\mathscr{A}^{-1}$, inverse of $\mathscr{A}$, (4.40) will be obtained, determining the n exergetic costs of the system.

$$B^* = \mathscr{A}^{-1} \cdot \Omega \tag{4.40}$$

The augmented matrix, which will be the base for the determination of the exergetic costs of the system's streams, must be square. In the case under study, simplified into two blocks, the incidence matrix is a (2 × 10) matrix, requiring an expansion with 8 additional equations. These equations determine the economic structure of the process. For the same physical reality, different economic realities may exist. For the determination of additional equations the order established in the previous sections will be followed, first identifying system wastes crossing the control surface. They are two, the exhaust gases from turbine, once they have yielded their exergy in the recovery steam generator (stream 93106) and the water returned to the environment after being used in the condensation subsystem (CCS) of the working fluid (stream 98103). The system resources are the gas turbine exhaust gases (stream 93103) and the flow of water used for condensing the working fluid (stream 98104). After identifying wastes and resources, there are ten unknowns for the streams and six equations (two of the incidence matrix and four from wastes and resources); therefore it is necessary to identify four additional equations. These are provided by the branchings, identified in the units with more than one output.

Table 4.2 Augmented matrix of the electricity generation system

Equations	93103	93106	94104	94107	98103	98104	W03	W04	W05	W06
HRSG	1	−1	1	−1	0	0	0	0	0	0
Turbine + CCS	0	0	−1	1	−1	1	−1	1	1	1
Resource 93103	1	0	0	0	0	0	0	0	0	0
Resource 98104	0	0	0	0	0	1	0	0	0	0
Waste 93106	0	1	0	0	0	0	0	0	0	0
Waste 98103	0	0	0	0	1	0	0	0	0	0
c_W03=c_W04	0	0	0	0	0	0	a	b	0	0
c_W03=c_W05	0	0	0	0	0	0	a	0	c	0
c_W03=c_W04	0	0	0	0	0	0	a	0	0	d
c_W03=c_94104	0	0	e	0	0	0	−a	0	0	0

a = 0.00026123 b = −0.004717
c = −0.029575789 d = −0.018044545
e = 1.00025×10^{-5}

(Streams)

The same unit exergetic cost is assigned to all electrical streams, i.e. the electricity generated in the steam turbine (stream W03-T971) will have the same unit exergetic cost as the electricity consumed by the CCS pumps (streams W04-P922, W05-P921, W06-P981), since some of the electricity generated is used to drive the pumps. For the additional equation needed, the same unit exergetic cost for the electricity generated by the turbine and stream 94104 will be assigned. The cost is, therefore, shared by the two outputs. This cost allocation has been done as, from a productive point of view, these streams are the main products of the turbine and CCS subsystem (as a whole). Therefore, there is a cost sharing between both of them proportional to their exergies. In this case, the gas turbine costs of the existing facility are not considered and therefore the cost of producing the exhaust gases (which is the input of the new facility) is equalled to zero. This will give the real cost of generating electricity with the new system, as it has been decoupled from a cost point of view. With the previous considerations, the augmented matrix would be as shown in Table 4.2.

For the construction of the assigned exergetic costs vector Ω, of dimension (10×1), the first two rows corresponding to the incidence matrix will be zero. The exergetic cost assigned to wastes will be zero. For resources, the assigned exergetic cost corresponds to the exergy of each current at the entrance of the system. For branchings, a zero will be assigned in this vector for each equation. The resulting assigned costs vector is shown in Table 4.3.

> The assigned cost vector of the whole system is contained in `cells B12:AH10` from the `workbook WB1011`.

Table 4.3 Assigned exergetic costs vector

	Ω
HRSG	0
Turbine + CCS	0
Resource 93103	11 818
Resource 98104	34 723
Waste 93106	0
Waste 98103	0
c_W03=c_W04	0
c_W03=c_W05	0
c_W03=c_W06	0
c_W03=c_94104	0

Table 4.4 Exergetic cost vector of the system

Stream	B^*
93103	11 818
93106	0
94104	1 319 300
94107	1 331 118
98103	0
98104	34 723
W03	50 516
W04	02 798
W05	446
W06	731

Once the incidence matrix has been completed and the assigned exergetic costs vector determined, the exergetic costs of all streams of the system can be determined by solving the system of Eq. 4.40.

Table 4.4 shows the exergetic costs of each stream of the system, and `cells B13:AH13` of `workbook WB1011`, gives the exergetic costs B^* of all the streams.

Once the exergetic cost has been calculated, the unit exergetic cost can also be determined (4.16): for the system under analysis, `cells B14:AH14` of `sheet MHBT (WB1011)` gives the unit exergetic costs of the streams.

Conclusions:

1. The determinant of the augmented matrix must not be 0 to solve the equations system. If the value is 0 the additional equations shall be revised, because at least one of the equations considered is a linear combination of the others.
2. As expected, the unit exergetic costs of all the resource inputs of the system are 1, because this condition has been set by (4.14).
3. As expected, the unit exergetic costs of the wastes are 0, because this condition has been set by (4.15).
4. Considering a fluid that is being continuously heated (94104, 94105, 94106, 94107), the exergetic cost continuously increases.
5. The highest unit exergetic cost is collected downstream of the system, by the electricity generated. This is the consequence of being the single product of the system: its exergetic cost equals the exergy of the resources of the whole installation (93103, 98104), its exergy is lower than the resource because the exergy destroyed in the equipment, as well as the exergy of the wastes.
6. The unit exergetic costs of products and resources for the equipment offers some interesting results. The relationship between the exergetic cost of the products and resources of a piece of equipment is also relevant ($\frac{\kappa_p^*}{\kappa_r^*} = \frac{\dot{B}_r}{\dot{B}_p}$ = unit consumption of the piece of equipment). The heat exchanger E916 has the greater unit consumption, because the exergy of the flue gases is collected by the product, a different approach has been followed by other authors [7].
7. The exergetic cost of the resources of the system, water (stream 98104) and exhaust gases from the gas turbine of the existing facility (stream 93103) is the exergy of the respective streams. As can be seen, the exergetic cost of wastes, exhaust gases after HRSG (stream 93106) and water after the CCS (stream 98103) is totally collected by the product (electricity produced by the turbine T971). The irreversibilities of the HRSG subsystem contribute to an exergetic cost increase of less than 1 % (exergy cost of stream 94107 compared to ingoing stream of the HRSG subsystem 94104). This case is a clear example of the conservative nature of the exergetic cost and how it increases as the stream goes through different pieces of equipment. When the branchings have been established, the exergetic cost of the electricity consumed by the pumps is proportional to the amount of exergy needed. Therefore the ratio between the amount of exergy needed by each pump (W04-P922, W05-P921 and W06-P981) the amount of exergy produced by the turbine (W03-T971) is maintained in the case of the exergetic costs of these work streams. If the productive structure of the system is changed, exergetic costs results would be different, depending on the decisions that are taken to represent the system (or subsystem).

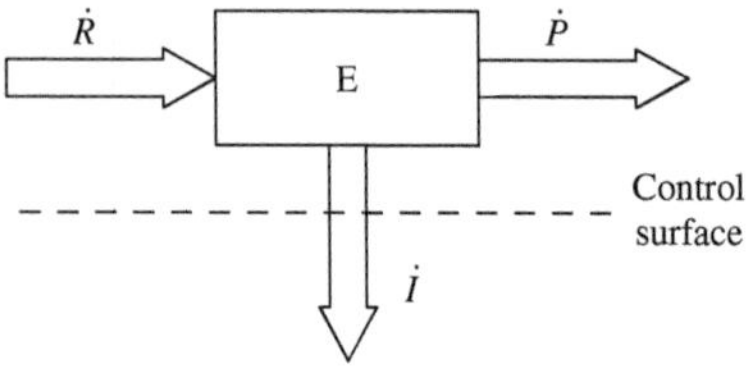

Fig. 4.10 Example of a piece of equipment

4.6 Performance and Ratios

The concepts of exergetic cost and resource/product allow general, clear and simple formulations of the efficiency with which a plant or facility transforms the resources it consumes into useful products (for example, a piece of equipment E of a plant, represented in Fig. 4.10).

According to (4.5), its exergy balance could be written as (4.41).

$$\dot{P} = \dot{R} - \left(\dot{I} + \dot{B}_d\right) \tag{4.41}$$

The *exergetic or rational efficiency* ζ of unit E is defined as (4.42)

$$\zeta \equiv \frac{\dot{P}}{\dot{R}} \tag{4.42}$$

According to (4.41), it verifies

$$\zeta = 1 - \frac{\dot{I} + \dot{B}_d}{\dot{R}} \leq 1 \tag{4.43}$$

Similarly, the unit exergetic consumption of E can be defined by (4.44), which fulfils (4.45) by applying (4.41):

$$\kappa \equiv \frac{\dot{R}}{\dot{P}} = \frac{1}{\zeta} \tag{4.44}$$

$$\kappa = 1 + \frac{\dot{I} + \dot{B}_d}{\dot{P}} \geq 1 \tag{4.45}$$

In the energetic assessment of a unit, the following ratios are generally helpful, giving a thorough quantitative image of the importance of exergy destruction and losses in a specific unit [1].

- *Exergy destruction ratio*:

$$r_d \equiv \frac{\dot{B}_d}{\dot{R}} \tag{4.46}$$

Table 4.5 Rational performance, destruction ratio and losses of the generation system

	R [kW]	P [kW]	I [kW]	Rational yield [%]	Exergy destruction efficiency [%]	Loss ratio (%)
HRSG	11 818	6 859	3 305	58	14	28
Turbine + CCS	141 557	103 803	35 371	73	2	25

- *Exergy loss ratio*:

$$r_I \equiv \frac{\dot{I}}{\dot{R}} \tag{4.47}$$

Moreover, if $\dot{P}$, $\dot{B}_d$ and $\dot{I}$ are eliminated between Eqs. 4.41, 4.42, 4.46 and 4.47, Eq. 4.52 is obtained, which shows a very intuitive connection between efficiency and performance ratios.

$$\zeta = 1 - r_I - r_d \tag{4.48}$$

If, as in Sect. 4.2, a distinction between waste and losses has been done, r_I would be restricted exclusively to waste and could be called *rejection ratio*. A loss ratio (4.49) could be also defined.

$$r_J \equiv \frac{\dot{J}}{\dot{R}} \tag{4.49}$$

Although the expressions for efficiency and ratios have been obtained for a single piece of equipment, they are also suitable for a complete system at the highest aggregation level.

Table 4.5 shows the results obtained for the rational efficiencies and ratios in the example case considered.

The rational efficiency of the turbine + CCS is higher than in the HRSG. The exergy destruction ratio and the losses ratio are higher in the HRSG.

4.7 Unit Exergetic Cost Build-Up

With the help of the R/P/I representation, it is possible to analyse in a thorough manner, how thermodynamic imperfections of a system intervene in the formation of exergetic costs of the equipment units that compose it. For a given piece of equipment i, its *unit exergetic costs of product and resource* can be defined by expressions (4.50) and (4.51). As the product and the resource can often comprise several streams, these formulas introduce single average values for the element in question. This will allow a simple general analysis [13].

$$\kappa^*_{P,i} \equiv \frac{P^*_i}{\dot{P}_i} \tag{4.50}$$

Table 4.6 Unit exergetic cost

Stream	Unit exergetic cost κ_i
93103	1.0
93106	0.0
94104	13.2
94107	12.5
98103	0.0
98104	1.0
W03	13.2
W04	13.2
W05	13.2
W06	13.2

$$\kappa^*_{R,i} \equiv \frac{R^*_i}{\dot{R}_i} \tag{4.51}$$

The exergetic cost balance is satisfied as the exergetic costs of wastes are zero:

$$P^*_i = R^*_i \tag{4.52}$$

Applying (4.50) and (4.51) the following expression can be written:

$$\kappa^*_{P,i}\dot{P}_i = \kappa^*_{R,i}\dot{R}_i \tag{4.53}$$

The exergy balance of a piece of equipment is expressed as follows:

$$\dot{R}_i = \dot{P}_i + \dot{I}_i + \dot{B}_{d,i} \tag{4.54}$$

with the help of (4.50) and (4.51)

$$\kappa^*_{P,i} = \kappa^*_{R,i}\left(1 + \frac{\dot{I}_i + \dot{B}_{d,i}}{\dot{P}_i}\right) \tag{4.55}$$

which indicates that, by cause of the destruction and loss of exergy in the piece of equipment, the unit exergetic cost of the product is always greater than that of the resource. The unit exergetic costs increase as resources are transformed into products in each unit [11].

Furthermore, from the formula (4.45) for the unit exergy consumption κ_i of a piece of equipment:

$$\kappa_i = 1 + \frac{\dot{I}_i + \dot{B}_{d,i}}{\dot{P}_i} \tag{4.56}$$

it is inferred by replacing (4.55) in (4.56).

Table 4.7 Unit exergetic cost and resource and product of each subsystem

	κ_R^*	κ_P^*	$\frac{\kappa_P^*}{\kappa_R^*}$
HRSG	1.00	1.72	1.72
Turbine + CCS	9.66	13.20	1.37

$$\kappa_{P,i}^* = \kappa_{R,i}^* \kappa_i \tag{4.57}$$

This equation relates the unit exergetic cost of the resources and the unit exergetic consumption of each piece of equipment within the system.

Table 4.6 shows the unit exergetic cost of all the streams of the system under analysis. It can be verified that the equations considered, as the unit exergetic cost of the inputs must be 1, the unit exergetic cost of the wastes 0, and all the power generation and consumption share the same unit exergetic cost.

Considering the R/P/I classification initially made, and the values obtained, the unit exergetic cost of resources and products that make up each subsystem can be obtained by highlighting their inefficiencies.

Table 4.7 shows the unit exergetic cost of resource and product of each subsystem and the ratio between them, which equals the exergy of the resources divided by the exergy of the products (the unit consumption of the zone).

The difference is the contribution of thermodynamic inefficiencies of each subsystem. It can be seen how the contribution of equipment to the exergetic cost of the products is greater, in the case of the HRSG.

References

1. Abdallah H (1999) Exergetic optimization of intercooled reheat chemically recuperated gas turbine. Energy Convers Manag 40:1679–1686
2. Lazzaretto A (2006) SPECO: a systematic and general methodology for calculating efficiencies and costs in thermal systems. Energy 31:1257–1289
3. Lozano MA (1993) Theory of exergetic cost and thermoeconomic optimization. In: Szagurt J, Kolenda Z, Tsatsaronis G, Ziebick A (eds) Proceedings of the international conference on energy system and ecology (ENSEC'93), vol 1, pp 339–50, Cracow, 5–9 July 1993
4. Montes JM et al (2009) Termoeconomía y optimizaci6n energ6tica (Thermoeconomics and energetic optimization). Fundaci6n G6mez Pardo y Consejo Superior de Ingenieros de Minas, Madrid. ISBN: 978-84-692-8320-2
5. Paulus DM (2006) Auxiliary equations for the determination of specific exergy revenues. Energy 31:3235–3247
6. Szargut J (2009) Utilization of the cryogenic exergy of liquid natural gas (LNG) for the production of electricity. Energy 34:827–837
7. Torres C, Valero A, Rangel V, Zaleta A (2006) On the cost formation process of the residues. Energy 33:144–152
8. Tsatsaronis G (2007) Definitions and nomenclature in exergy analysis and exergoeconomics. Energy 32:249–253
9. Valero A (1987) The exergetic cost and related concepts: an application to a simple cogeneration plant, ASME. In: Moran MJ, Sciubba E (eds) Second law analysis of thermal systems. ASME Book No. I00236, New York, pp 123–130

10. Valero A (1990) On causality in organized energy systems. Part II. Symbolic exergoeconomis. In: Stecco SS, Moran MJ (eds) International symposium: a future for energy. Pergamon Press, Florence, pp 393–401
11. Valero A (1994) Application of the exergetic cost theory to the CGAM problem. Energy 19(3):365–381
12. Valero A (1996) On-line monitoring of power plant performance, using exergetic cost techniques. Appl Therm Eng 16(12):933–948
13. Valero A (2005) Structural theory and thermoeconomic diagnosis. Part II: application to an actual power plant. Energy Convers Manag 43:1247–1266
14. Valero A (2006) Exergy accounting: capabilities and drawbacks. Energy 31:164–180

Chapter 5
Thermoeconomic Cost

Abstract This chapter gives the theoretical background for the development and execution of thermoeconomic balances of systems, and applies it to the example case. Once the thermoeconomic balance is set up, a brief description of the fixed and variable costs is given, and their calculation is applied to the system. Thermoeconomic costs are determined and related cost increases show how thermoeconomic analysis will serve to analyse industrial systems, as can be seen when applied to the example system. Finally, the exergoeconomic factor is defined and applied.

5.1 Introduction

Any kind of stream, material or not, carries an exergetic flow $\dot{B}_j$ and has an exergetic cost B_j^*, both expressible in power units, for example, in kW. Now a thermoeconomic cost $\dot{\Pi}_j$ will be assigned to each stream, which is defined as its *economic production cost*, or *cost flow*, expressed in monetary units per unit of time, such as € s^{-1}. Since the exergetic cost $\dot{B}_j$ measures the exergy consumed to produce the stream j, the ratio between the thermoeconomic cost $\dot{\Pi}_j$ and the exergetic cost will represent *the economic cost* c_j^* per unit of exergy consumed in the production of the stream, Eq. 5.1, where c_j^* is known as the *unit thermoeconomic cost* and is expressed in monetary units per unit of exergy, such as € kJ^{-1}.

$$c_j^* \equiv \frac{\dot{\Pi}_j}{B_j^*} \tag{5.1}$$

In a facility that uses a single resource, these ideas have a clear practical meaning. The (dimensionless) unit exergetic cost κ_j^* measure the unit resource consumption (kJ of fuel exergy per kJ of stream exergy) and the unit thermoeconomic cost c_j^* represents the unit cost of the resource € kJ^{-1} [8]. In a similar way unit exergoeconomic cost

E. Querol et.al., *Practical Approach to Exergy and Thermoeconomic Analyses of Industrial Processes*, SpringerBriefs in Energy,
DOI: 10.1007/978-1-4471-4622-3_5, © The Author(s) 2013

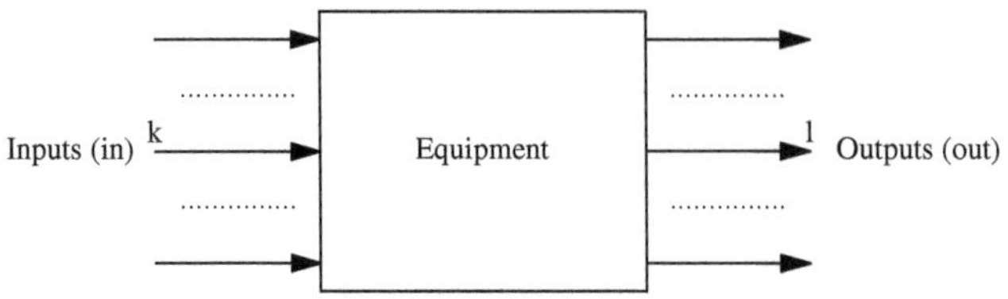

Fig. 5.1 System at maximum aggregation level with various inputs and outputs

c_j, Eq. 5.2 is the economic cost of the unit of exergy of a stream j:

$$c_j \equiv \frac{\dot{\Pi}_j}{\dot{B}_j} \tag{5.2}$$

From (5.1), (5.2) and (4.16), a link between the three unit costs is obtained.

$$\dot{\Pi}_j = c_j^* B_j^* = c_j \dot{B}_j = c_j^* \left(\kappa_j^* \dot{B}_j\right) \tag{5.3}$$

$$c_j = \kappa_j^* c_j^* \tag{5.4}$$

Definitions (5.1) and (5.2) provide two equivalent ways to relate the thermoeconomic cost of a stream with the exergy needed to produce it (c_j^*), or with the exergy of the stream (c_j). In any case, thermodynamics is going to provide a thorough and unambiguous connection between exergy and economy, regardless of any accounting convention.

5.2 Thermoeconomic Balance

If a system at its maximum aggregation level is considered (as in Fig. 5.1), with various inputs and outputs, a vertical economic balance must express that the total cost of the outputs equals the total cost of the inputs, plus the fixed costs of depreciation, maintenance, operating and overhead costs of the plant, all per unit time.

The total amount of fixed costs flow is represented by $\dot{Z}$ and hereinafter designated as *fixed cost*. Therefore, the following balance may be written:

$$\sum_k \dot{\Pi}_{ik} + \dot{Z} = \sum_l \dot{\Pi}_{ol} \tag{5.5}$$

Matrix expression where the row matrix $A_{(1\times n)}$ is the same one used for mass or energy balances, defining the physical reality of the system.

$$A_{(1\times n)} \cdot \Pi_{(n\times 1)} + \dot{Z} = 0 \tag{5.6}$$

The vector $\Pi_{(n\times 1)}$ (5.7) is named *thermoeconomic cost vector*, resembling the energy, exergy and exergetic cost vectors.

$$\Pi_{(n\times 1)} \equiv \begin{bmatrix} \vdots \\ \dot{\Pi}_{ik} \\ \vdots \\ \dot{\Pi}_{ol} \end{bmatrix} \tag{5.7}$$

This formulation is easily extended to lower aggregation levels, so that the general matrix expression of the *economic balance* of a system consisting of m connected items by n streams remains as in (5.8) where $A_{(m\times n)}$ is the incidence matrix defined in Sect. 3.2, $\dot{\Pi}_{(n\times 1)}$ the *thermoeconomic cost vector* and $Z_{(m\times 1)}$ the *fixed cost vector* $\dot{Z}_i$ of the system [4].

$$A_{(m\times n)} \cdot \Pi_{(n\times 1)} + Z_{(m\times 1)} = 0_{(m\times 1)} \tag{5.8}$$

As in the case of exergetic costs, the (5.8) balance provides m equations with $n > m$ unknowns and therefore additional $n - m$ equations are needed, as when performing the exergetic cost balance. These additional equations are obtained by the same procedure described in Sects. 4.4 and 4.5.

The balance expressed by (5.8) has been formulated on a strictly economic basis, without resorting to thermodynamics. The latter will be used to formulate the additional equations when dealing with branchings.

The additional equations are formulated using the following criteria:

(a) *Inputs.* Its thermoeconomic cost $\dot{\Pi}_{in}$ equals the *cost flow* of the stream ϕ_{in}:

$$\dot{\Pi}_{in} \equiv \phi_{in} \tag{5.9}$$

When applying (5.1) and (5.2) in the expression (5.9), (5.10) can be written.

$$\dot{\Pi}_{in} \equiv \phi_{in} = c^*_{in} B^*_{in} = c_{in} \dot{B}_{in} \tag{5.10}$$

and according to (4.14)

$$B^*_{in} = \dot{B}_{in} \quad ; \quad \kappa^*_{in} = 1 \quad ; \quad c_{in} = c^*_{in} \tag{5.11}$$

In the case under analysis, two resources are employed in the system: the flue gases 93103, which have been considered to have a cost of 0 € s^{-1} and the condensation water 98104, with an estimated cost of 0.00001 € kg^{-1}, provided by the treatment needed by the water, because the pumping needs are already considered in P981.

It is interesting to point out the influence of the economic decisions in the results obtained. If the flue gases 93103 share the cost of the turbo compressor from the natural gas station, instead of considering it free, then the power generated

Table 5.1 Unit value of defined thermoeconomic costs

Concept	Unit value [€ kg^{-1}]
Water	0.00001
Exhaust gases	0

Table 5.2 Defined thermoeconomic costs of system resources

Concept	$\phi_{(n-m)\times 1}$ [€ s^{-1}]
Water (98104)	0.002
Exhaust gases (93103)	0

by that compressor will be cheaper, but the cost of the electricity generated by the proposed system would be greater. A most rational decision is to distribute the cost, if the installation is considered as a whole from the beginning, and consider the flue gases free if the project consist on using a waste (the flue gases) from an existing installation, because the benefits of the project (the electricity generated) shall be analysed against the installation cost, to decide whether it is in their interests or not to afford the new installation. Whatever the decision made, as the calculations are made with a workbook, it is easy and convenient to show both results and discuss the possibilities.

In the system under consideration, the resources are air, gas turbine exhaust and water (it was considered that the compressor station is located near a water source: sea water, a river...). For each of them, the unit value of the thermoeconomic costs have been estimated as shown in Table 5.1. The assigned cost for exhaust gases exiting from the compression station gas turbine has been considered zero. To determine the thermoeconomic costs, unit values in Table 5.1 must be multiplied by their mass flows. As resources, the amount of these streams needed will vary with the amount of working hours per year considered for this facility. As the cost of these resources vary with the production hours, they can be considered as variable costs... In this case the thermoeconomic costs remain as shown in (the corresponding current is shown in parentheses) Table 5.2.

(b) *By-products*. Just as in Sect. 4.4, thermoeconomic cost $\dot{\Pi}_b$ can be assigned to it, equal to the one they would have with the best available specific process ϕ_b [€ s^{-1}]. Therefore, for a given by-product b:

$$\dot{\Pi}_b \equiv \phi_b \tag{5.12}$$

(c) *Waste*. As noted in Sect. 4.4, in terms of its exergetic cost:

$$\dot{\Pi}_r \equiv 0 \tag{5.13}$$

Two wastes are found in the installation: the exhaust gases 93106, and the condensation water 98103. It must be remembered that this equation does not affirm that the cost of the residues is 0, but that the cost of the residues shall be collected by the products (the electricity generated).

(d) *Branchings.* As in Sect. 4.4, in the case of an internal branching of two main products, there can be assigned the same *unit thermoeconomic cost* c^* to both currents. By having the same *unit exergetic cost* κ, according to Sect. 4.4, Eq. 5.3 indicates that this will also occur with the unit exergoeconomic cost. Therefore, both (5.14) and (5.15) are fulfilled [7].

$$\frac{\dot{\Pi}_j}{B_j^*} = \frac{\dot{\Pi}_k}{B_k^*} \tag{5.14}$$

$$\frac{\dot{\Pi}_j}{\dot{B}_j} = \frac{\dot{\Pi}_k}{\dot{B}_k} \tag{5.15}$$

It must be noted that conditions (a), (b) and (c) are merely economic and that the only one that is thermodynamic in nature is condition (d), referring to branchings. In order to make use of the same augmented matrix, Eq. 5.15 is used instead of (5.14), allowing the determination of the thermoeconomic costs without the need of calculating the exergetic costs of the streams needed by (5.14).

As it was shown in Sect. 4.5, under these conditions it is provided the exact $n - m$ number of additional equations that, in conjunction with the m of system (5.8), complete the total n needed to determine the n thermoeconomic costs of the system. The same economic matrix $\alpha_{(n-m)\times n}$ is introduced, and the defined thermoeconomic costs vector, $\phi_{(n-m)\times 1}$ is created, whose elements have the following values:

- *Inputs*: ϕ_{in}
- *By-products*: ϕ_b
- *Waste*: 0
- *Branchings*: 0

The additional $n - m$ equations will be represented through matrices, as follows.

$$\alpha_{(n-m)\times n} \cdot \Pi_{(n\times 1)} = \phi_{(n-m)\times 1} \tag{5.16}$$

The complete system will be

$$\left.\begin{aligned} A_{(m\times n)} \cdot \Pi_{(n\times 1)} + Z_{(m\times 1)} &= 0_{(m\times 1)} \\ \alpha_{(n-m)\times n} \cdot \Pi_{(n\times 1)} - \phi_{(n-m)\times 1} &= 0_{(n-m)\times 1} \end{aligned}\right\} \tag{5.17}$$

Introducing the augmented matrix $\mathscr{A}_{(n\times n)}$, of Sect. 4.5, and defining with (5.18) vector $\Phi_{(n\times 1)}$, named the *assigned thermoeconomic cost vector*:

$$\Phi_{(n\times 1)} \equiv \begin{bmatrix} Z \\ \cdots \\ -\phi \end{bmatrix} \tag{5.18}$$

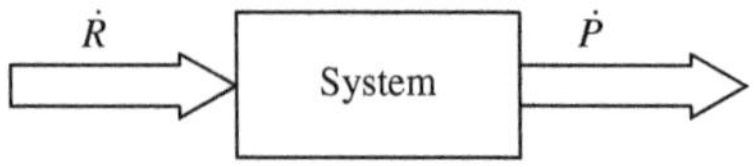

Fig. 5.2 Diagram of a system at the highest aggregation level

the *thermoeconomic balance* (5.19) can be written in the form:

$$\mathscr{A}_{(n\times n)} \cdot \Pi_{(n\times 1)} + \Phi_{(n\times 1)} = 0_{(n\times 1)} \qquad (5.19)$$

For the determination of the thermoeconomic cost of a system, it is necessary to set the defined thermoeconomic costs by the criteria previously outlined. For the construction of the defined thermoeconomic cost vector, $\phi_{(n-m)\times 1}$, it is sufficient to introduce the cost of the used resources, considering the maximum aggregation level, i.e. solely considering the resources crossing the control surface of the whole system. Therefore, it is quite simple to calculate the thermoeconomic costs of the streams, as only the cost of the resources and fixed costs are needed (which are surely known or can be easily estimated), the same augmented matrix is used, so only a new operation shall be made in the workbook.

In the practical case, the augmented matrix is in `sheet A`, the assigned thermoeconomic cost vector is located in `MHBT!A15`.

5.3 Fixed and Variable Costs

A productive system to the highest level of aggregation is sketched in Fig. 5.2, generating the product $\dot{P}$ consuming resource $\dot{R}$. The following economic balance (5.20) will be verified, according to (5.5), where $\dot{Z}$ is the flow of the system's fixed cost. This cost ($\dot{Z}$), although it varies with the working hours of the facility is indeed an internal cost of the process that does not vary with the price variation of the resources consumed by the system, and is generated by the capital invested and the operating and maintenance costs, among others.

$$\dot{\Pi}_P = \dot{Z} + \dot{\Pi}_R \qquad (5.20)$$

With a similar reasoning to that in Sect. 4.7 for unit exergetic costs, *unit exergoeconomic costs of product and resource* may be introduced through expressions (5.21) and (5.22), with the same form as (5.2):

$$c_P \equiv \frac{\dot{\Pi}_P}{\dot{P}} \qquad (5.21)$$

$$c_R \equiv \frac{\dot{\Pi}_R}{\dot{R}} \tag{5.22}$$

Since product and resource may be composed by several streams, these definitions introduce single values that, as reasoned in Sect. 4.7, will simplify the analysis. Using (5.21), (5.22) and (4.44), (5.23) is obtained where κ is the unit consumption of the system.

$$\dot{\Pi}_R = c_R \dot{R} = \kappa c_R \dot{P} \tag{5.23}$$

And if substituted in (5.20), (5.24) is attained. The last term, proportional to $\dot{P}$, expresses the *variable cost* of the product.

$$\dot{\Pi}_P = \dot{Z} + \kappa c_R \dot{P} \tag{5.24}$$

If (5.21), (5.22) are applied to obtain the unit costs, (5.25) is obtained, which shows that the *unit variable cost* is constant and the *unit fixed cost* is inversely proportional to the production level.

$$c_P = \frac{\dot{Z}}{\dot{P}} + \kappa c_R \tag{5.25}$$

Equations 5.24 and 5.25 are expressions of a *lineal model of production costs*, customarily used in the economic analysis of industrial processes. In making investment decisions, there is an interesting comparison between fixed and variable costs. Generally, simple technologies tend to have low fixed costs, while variable costs are high upon consuming resources in an inefficient manner and are, therefore, resource intensive.

Advanced technologies, however, improve the utilization of resources and have lower variable costs, but its fixed costs are greater owing to their complexity and the use of more expensive equipment and are therefore capital intensive [6] and the equipment fixed cost.

Figure 5.3 represents a typical situation, in which a simple technology 1 is compared to another, 2, which is more capital intensive. Fixed cost FC1 of the first one is less than the FC2 of the second one. The contrary occurs with their respective *unit variable costs*. For productions less than the *equivalence* or *break-even* point, Technology 1 is preferable from an economic point of view. Above it, however, the less expensive one is Technology 2. It should be noted here that the *exergetic cost*, defined in Sect. 4.3, is a purely *variable cost*.

5.4 Variable Thermoeconomic Costs

It is interesting to compare the assigned exergetic cost vector Ω (4.38), with the assigned thermoeconomic vector Φ (5.18). The first m elements of the first one are zero, while those of the second one take the $\dot{Z}_i$ values of fixed costs. This is caused

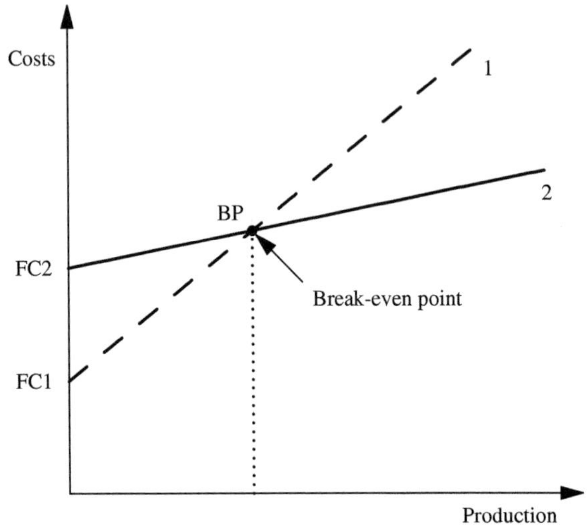

Fig. 5.3 Cost break-even point

by the fact that the exergetic costs calculated with (4.39) are variable, whereas the thermoeconomic costs calculated with (5.19) are, on the contrary, total. The variable thermoeconomic costs can be easily determined. It is sufficient to apply the matrix expression (5.19), substituting vector (5.26), formally analogous to the vector Ω defined by (4.38), for vector Φ. The first m elements are zero, since now there are no fixed costs assigned. If there were a by-product, the variable cost would have to be assigned to ϕ_b.

$$\Phi^{\text{var}}_{(n\times 1)} \equiv \begin{bmatrix} 0_{(m\times 1)} \\ \cdots \\ -\phi_{(n-m)\times 1} \end{bmatrix} \tag{5.26}$$

The thermoeconomic balance (5.19) could be written as (5.27), which has the same form as the *exergetic cost balance* (4.39).

$$\mathscr{A}_{(n\times n)} \cdot \Pi_{(n\times 1)} = -\Phi^{\text{var}}_{(n\times 1)} \tag{5.27}$$

The results obtained with both balances are not always equivalent, since both vectors are not generally proportional and it is not possible to go from one to the other by multiplication by a scalar. In effect, the unit exergoeconomic costs c_e of the inputs do not have to be the same, in the way that (5.10) does not always yield values ϕ_{in} proportional to $\dot{B}_{in}$.

However, there are cases in which $-\Phi^{\text{var}}_{(n\times 1)}$ and $\Omega_{(n\times 1)}$ are proportional; this occurs, for example, when there is a single resource and no by-products, as in many thermal power plants.

5.5 Fixed Cost Calculation

To calculate the thermoeconomic costs by the balance (5.8), the assigned thermoeconomic costs vector $\Phi_{(n\times 1)}$ (5.18) is required. Vector ϕ can be already determined but if the fixed costs $\dot{Z}$ are not known, a preliminary approximation should be used.

The fixed cost flow $\dot{Z}$ of a complete facility can be decomposed in the investment cost flow $\dot{Z}^I$ and the Operation and Maintenance cost flow $\dot{Z}^{OM}$, as described in (5.28).

$$\dot{Z} = \dot{Z}^I + \dot{Z}^{OM} \tag{5.28}$$

The terms of (5.28) can be estimated as follows in order to obtain a first approach to the thermoeconomic analysis of the system.

(a) *Flow of operation and maintenance cost* ($\dot{Z}^{OM}$). Those of maintenance and operation (O&M) are determined separately. In preliminary analyses, maintenance cost can be estimated to be between 2 and 10 % of total investment and 6 % may be a reasonable initial estimate. As for the cost of operation, in simple cases it is usually based on the cost of personnel (which can be considered from 30000 to 50000 €/(empl.·year). For example, for a small power plant it would be 2.5 empl./shift, in this case, the total workforce would be expressed by (5.29).

$$\frac{24\ (\text{h/day}) \times 7\ (\text{day/week}) \times 2.5\ (\text{empl./shift})}{38\ (\text{h/week} \cdot \text{shift})} = 11\ \text{empl.} \tag{5.29}$$

Moreover, depending on the standpoint of the user, additional overhead costs could be added (structure costs, company overheads, etc.).
The operation and maintenance factor can be calculated as soon as the annual cost of operation and maintenance OM_{TOT} has been estimated. This factor is defined as the annual O&M cost per unit of capital invested TCI.

$$f_{\text{OM}} \equiv \frac{OM_{\text{TOT}}}{\text{TCI}} \tag{5.30}$$

(b) *Investment cost flow* ($\dot{Z}^I$). One must begin by estimating the *total capital investment* (TCI). Table 5.3 makes a possible breakdown, in which the percentages given are typical rounded values that can vary in each considered particular situation. The TCI/PEC relationship between total capital investment TCI and total purchased equipment cost PEC is usually called the installation or Lang factor. Generally a same value is approximated for facilities of a certain type. Knowing this value, the total investment can be simply estimated by multiplying the purchased equipment cost by that factor. It is possible to obtain a better approximation by making use of a specific installation factor for the different items comprised by a given facility. Plenty of data exists for the $\text{IEC}_i/\text{PEC}_i$, which allow the estimation of a specific IEC_i for each device. Total installed

Table 5.3 Estimated total capital investment

		%	Cumulative %
Purchased equipment cost (PEC)		100	100
Installation direct cost			
Material	70		
Labor	50	120	
Installation indirect cost			
Transportation and insurance	30		
Engineering and supervision	40		
General costs of installation	10	80	
Installation costs		200	
Installed equipment cost (IEC)			300
Contingency	30		
Startup	10		
Financial charges	10		
Other costs		50	
Total capital investment (TCI)			350

equipment cost IEC of the facility is obtained by adding the obtained values and, from that point, the calculations continue as indicated in Table 5.3.

It should be borne in mind the considerable differences between total equipment cost (PEC) and total capital investment (TCI). As can be seen in the example of Table 5.3, when an addition to an existing plant is analysed the total investment can more than triple the equipment cost. Forgetting this can lead to serious errors in thermoeconomic analyses. Once the total investment is estimated, the *equivalent annualized cost* will have to be calculated through (5.31) where $\frac{A}{P_{i,n}}$, Eq. 5.32, represents the *capital recovery factor*:

$$A_{\mathrm{TOT}} = \mathrm{TCI} \cdot \frac{A}{P_{i,n}} \tag{5.31}$$

$$\frac{A}{P_{i,n}} = \frac{i(1+i)^n}{(1+i)^n - 1} \tag{5.32}$$

In this expression, i is the per unit capital cost and n is the planned life of the facility (in years). Equation 5.31 determines the equivalent uniform annuity to the total investment. The total annual fixed cost flow will verify, in accordance with (5.30) and (5.31):

$$\mathrm{FC}_{\mathrm{TOT}} = A_{\mathrm{TOT}} + \mathrm{OM}_{\mathrm{TOT}} = \left(\frac{A}{P_{i,n}} + f_{\mathrm{OM}}\right) \mathrm{TCI} \tag{5.33}$$

Table 5.4 Cost of installed equipment

Subsystem	PEC 1987 [$]	IEC 1987 [$]
HRSG	5.76×10^4	1.95×10^5
Turbine + CCS	1.35×10^6	4.39×10^6
System	1.41×10^6	4.59×10^6

The annual fixed cost flow of a given piece of equipment j can be determined in proportion to its acquisition cost PEC_j as follows

$$\text{FC}_j = \text{FC}_{\text{TOT}} \cdot \frac{\text{PEC}_j}{\text{PEC}_{\text{TOT}}} \tag{5.34}$$

The costs obtained this way are annual costs, which shall be divided by the equivalent annual operating time at full power per year, usually expressed in h/year. For a utilization factor of 100 %, the annual operating time will be 365 day/year × 24 h/day = 8 760 h/year. The fixed cost flow of each piece of equipment j can be obtained with (5.35) where OT is the annual operating time, generally expressed in h/year. In this case, 6 800 h have been considered, which means aprox. 78 % of the year.

$$\dot{Z}_j = \frac{FC_j}{\text{OT}} \tag{5.35}$$

To calculate the fixed costs of each piece of equipment there are two options:

(a) Using former known costs.
(b) Estimate the costs of every piece of equipment with the help of existing literature. In this case, calculations of their costs in terms of their most characteristic properties must be done.

In the case analysed, the costs of every unit have been estimated [1], and results in Table 5.4 are achieved for the considered subsystems.

To determine these costs, the equipment acquisition cost (EAC) has been estimated, taking into account the installation cost (IEC) of the above mentioned, considering that the installation means an increase of 2.25 times. Having once determined said cost, the total investment cost in the existing plant is calculated, for which it means that the aforementioned is 1.33 times the installed equipment cost (IEC). After determining the cost with the method exposed, which gives estimates in 1987 currency ($), this value can be updated to the most recent currency available [5] being its value in euros, applying an exchange rate of 0.8 € $\$^{-1}$.

Once the total investment is determined, it will be necessary to determine the annualized equivalent cost through the equivalent uniform annuity, as well as the operation and maintenance cost to obtain the annualized fixed cost.

For this calculation, the hypotheses in Table 5.5 have been considered.

Using these values, the different components of the total fixed cost, as well as total fixed cost, are shown in Table 5.6, where FC [€ year^{-1}] is the total annualized fixed cost for the complete system.

Table 5.5 Cost of capital, useful life and operation and maintenance factor

Data	Value
Cost of capital [i]	4 %
Useful life	20 years
O&M factor	3 %
OT	6 800 h year^{-1}

Table 5.6 Total fixed cost and its components

Data	Value
TCI/CAE	2.50
TCI [€]	8 685 589.59
$\frac{A}{P_{i,n}}$ [year^{-1}]	0.07
A_{TOT} [€ year^{-1}]	639 100.89
O&M [€ year^{-1}]	260 567.69
FC [€ year^{-1}]	899 668.57

Table 5.7 Annualized fixed costs vector

Subsystem	Z [€ s^{-1}]
HRSG	2.90×10^{-3}
Turbine + CCS	3.36×10^{-2}
System	3.65×10^{-2}

If it is considered that the facility will work 6 800 h/year, and the value of the fixed cost of the system is distributed between subsystems in terms of the equipment acquisition cost, the fixed costs vector results as shown in Table 5.7.

After determining the fixed cost of the equipment, the complete thermoeconomic analysis of the system can be done considering the fixed and variable costs of the system.

As the variable costs are almost zero in the case of the exhaust gases and not significant if compared to the equipment cost, the cost per MWh generated will almost be the investment cost per MWh.

5.6 Thermoeconomic Cost Buildup

Following the R/P formulation, the economic balance of a piece of equipment unit i of a specific system can be expressed as follows

$$\dot{\Pi}_{P,i} = \dot{\Pi}_{R,i} + \dot{Z}_i \tag{5.36}$$

To introduce the *unit exergoeconomic costs of product and resource* of the equipment at issue definitions, (5.21) and (5.22) must be applied with the following results:

$$c_{P,i} \equiv \frac{\dot{\Pi}_{P,i}}{\dot{P}_i} \tag{5.37}$$

$$c_{R,i} \equiv \frac{\dot{\Pi}_{R,i}}{\dot{R}_i} \tag{5.38}$$

By applying these formulas to (5.36), the following result is obtained:

$$c_{P,i}\dot{P}_i = c_{R,i}\dot{R}_i + \dot{Z}_i \tag{5.39}$$

And solving for the unit exergoeconomic cost of the product.

$$c_{P,i} = \frac{c_{R,i}\dot{R}_i + \dot{Z}_i}{\dot{P}_i} \tag{5.40}$$

To evaluate the effect of exergy destruction on any piece of equipment, $\dot{R}_i$ must be replaced by its value given by the exergy balance (4.9):

$$c_{P,i} = \frac{c_{R,i}\left(\dot{P}_i + \dot{I}_i + \dot{B}_{d,i}\right) + \dot{Z}_i}{\dot{P}_i} = c_{R,i} + \frac{c_{R,i}\left(\dot{I}_i + \dot{B}_{d,i}\right)}{\dot{P}_i} + \frac{\dot{Z}_i}{\dot{P}_i} \tag{5.41}$$

The last member of this expression indicates that the unit exergoeconomic cost of the resource is increased for the product by the waste $\dot{I}_i$, and exergy destruction $\dot{B}_{d,i}$ and the equipment fixed cost $\dot{Z}_i$ [2, 3].

The cost increase originated in equipment i can be represented by means of a dimensionless factor r_i, named *relative cost increase*, as follows.

$$r_i \equiv \frac{c_{P,i} - c_{R,i}}{c_{R,i}} \tag{5.42}$$

This factor is very useful in the iterative optimization of an equipment unit.

If, for example, resource cost suffers an increase between two steps, one should try to minimize the relative cost increase and not the unit exergoeconomic cost of the product. If (5.41) is applied to (5.42), it gives:

$$r_i = \frac{\dot{I}_i + \dot{B}_{d,i}}{\dot{P}_i} + \frac{\dot{Z}_i}{c_{R,i}\dot{P}_i} \tag{5.43}$$

An appreciable simplification is achieved by making use of the unit *exergy consumption* κ_i of the equipment, given by (5.44), which transforms (5.43) in an expressive manner reflecting the contributions of the inefficiencies of the equipment and its fixed costs to the relative cost increase.

$$r_i = \kappa_i - 1 + \frac{\dot{Z}_i}{c_{R,i}\dot{P}_i} \tag{5.44}$$

Table 5.8 Thermoeconomic costs

Stream	Π [€ s^{-1}]
93103	0.0000
93106	0.0000
94104	0.4924
94107	0.4953
98103	0.0000
98104	0.0020
W03	0.0413
W04	0.0023
W05	0.0004
W06	0.0006

If instead of the unit consumption the exergetic performance $\zeta_i = \frac{1}{\kappa_i}$ is to be used, the following result is obtained, which is equally useful:

$$r_i = \frac{1 - \zeta_i}{\zeta_i} + \frac{\dot{Z}_i}{c_{R,i} \dot{P}_i} \tag{5.45}$$

Following an R/P/I classification initially defined for each one of the subsystems that form part of the electricity generation system under analysis, the exergoeconomic costs of the products, resources, wastes and destroyed exergy are determined.

Once fixed and variables costs and the system's augmented matrix have been calculated, the thermoeconomic costs of the different streams of the system can be determined. Table 5.8 shows the thermoeconomic costs for all the streams contained in the system.

Once the thermoeconomic costs and the exergy of the different streams are determined, the unit exergoeconomic costs of the electricity generation [€ MWh^{-1}] can be calculated. In this case, the exergoeconomic cost of the electricity is given at the exit of the turbine.

In this case the exergoeconomic cost is 64.91 € MWh^{-1}. If the cost of generating electricity with the gas turbine has to be considered, the cost of the electricity generated by this system will be 113.2 € MWh^{-1}, being the contribution of the compression station system 42.65 % of the total cost. Table 5.9 shows the results obtained. The contribution of the cost of losses is negligible compared with the cost of exergy destruction (Eq. 4.52).

Table 5.10 shows the absolute and relative cost increases for each of the subsystems. It is noted that the greatest contribution to the absolute cost increase occurs in the turbine + CCS. In all cases, the cost increases due to the inefficiency of each subsystem or destruction of exergy outweigh the losses. The determination of these costs, caused by destruction and losses of exergy, shows the advantage of using thermoeconomic on conventional economic analysis, since in the latter, such costs would remain hidden.

Table 5.9 Exergy and costs for each subsystem according to R/P/I classification

Subsystem	R	B_R [kW]	Π_R [€ s^{-1}]	c_R [€ MWh^{-1}]
HRSG	93103	11 818.08	0.00	0.00
Turbine + CCS	W04+W05+W06+ 98104+94107	141 557.18	0.50	12.73
Subsystem	P	B_P [kW]	Π_P [€ s^{-1}]	c_P [€ MWh^{-1}]
HRSG	94107-94104	6 859.43	0.00	1.52
Turbine + CCS	94104+W03-T971	103 802.86	0.53	18.51
Subsystem	I	B_I [kW]	Π_I [€ s^{-1}]	
HRSG	93106	3 304.75	0.000	
Turbine + CCS	98103	35 370.51	0.125	
Subsystem		B_d [kW]	Π_{B_d} [€ s^{-1}]	
HRSG		1 654.00	0.000	
Turbine + CCS		2 384	0.008	

Table 5.10 Absolute and relative cost increases owing to each subsystem

Subsystem	Π_c [€ s^{-1}]	c [°/1]
HRSG	0.003	Infinite
Turbine + CCS	0.167	0.454

From the standpoint of relative cost increases, the main improvements should be made upon the HRSG, but considering absolute increases, the opposite is concluded. The exergoeconomic factor will indicate what type of improvements should be made within each subsystem.

5.7 Exergoeconomic Factor

Based on the exergy balance expressed by (4.9), the following expression is obtained.

$$\dot{\Pi}_{R,i} = c_{R,i}\dot{R}_i = c_{R,i}\left(\dot{P}_i + \dot{I}_i + \dot{B}_{d,i}\right) \tag{5.46}$$

and substituting into (5.36),

$$\dot{\Pi}_{P,i} = c_{P,i}\dot{P}_i = c_{R,i}\dot{P}_i + c_{R,i}\left(\dot{I}_i + \dot{B}_{d,i}\right) + \dot{Z}_i \tag{5.47}$$

expressing the thermoeconomic cost of the product in terms of the thermoeconomic cost $c_{R,i}\dot{P}_i$ that the product would have, if its unit exergoeconomic cost $c_{P,i}$ were the same as that of the resource $c_{R,i}$, and of the thermodynamic cost increases (destruction and loss of exergy) and of the economic ones (fixed costs). The $(\dot{\Pi}_{P,i} - c_{R,i}\dot{P}_i)$ difference is named *absolute cost increase* of the equipment:

$$\dot{\Pi}_{c,i} \equiv c_{R,i}\left(\dot{I}_i + \dot{B}_{d,i}\right) + \dot{Z}_i \tag{5.48}$$

In it, the two contributions to the cost increase can be seen:

- Thermodynamic: $c_{R,i}\left(\dot{I}_i + \dot{B}_{d,i}\right)$
- Economic: Fixed cost $\dot{Z}_i$

The thermodynamic contribution may be subdivided into two parts:

- The product $c_{R,i}\dot{I}_i$, named *cost of exergy loss*, is a cost flow (monetary amount by unit of time) like $\dot{Z}_i$:

$$\dot{\Pi}_{I,i} \equiv c_{R,i}\dot{I}_i \tag{5.49}$$

- The product $c_{R,i}\dot{B}_{d,i}$, named *cost of exergy destruction*:

$$\dot{\Pi}_{d,i} \equiv c_{R,i}\dot{B}_{d,i} \tag{5.50}$$

In both cases, they are hidden costs, because they do not explicitly appear in cost accounting. Taking (5.48), (5.49) and (5.50) into account, (5.51) is obtained.

$$\dot{\Pi}_{c,i} \equiv \dot{\Pi}_{I,i} + \dot{\Pi}_{d,i} + \dot{Z}_i \tag{5.51}$$

In the thermoeconomic analysis of the piece of equipment, it would interest one to know the relative importance of the thermodynamic and economic contribution to the cost increase. This is achieved through the *exergoeconomic factor*, which is defined as the ratio of the economic cost increase, owing to the fixed cost, and the total cost increase.

$$f_i \equiv \frac{\dot{Z}_i}{\dot{\Pi}_{I,i} + \dot{\Pi}_{d,i} + \dot{Z}_i} = \frac{\dot{Z}_i}{c_{R,i}\left(\dot{I}_i + \dot{B}_{d,i}\right) + \dot{Z}_i} \tag{5.52}$$

This gives a measure of the relative contribution of fixed costs to the total cost increase originated in the equipment. If the exergoeconomic factor is small, an improvement in the product cost could be achieved by increasing the thermodynamic efficiency of the equipment, although this would require an incremental investment in the piece of equipment, with a consequent increase in fixed costs. If, on the contrary, the exergoeconomic factor is high, it would be appropriate to simplify the design for reducing the equipment cost even incurring on a greater destruction of exergy. Generally, each basic type of equipment has a typical f_i range, as indicated in Table 5.11.

The equipment with higher absolute cost increases will be the first ones to search for feasible design improvements, paying special attention to those with high *relative cost increase* r_i. The *exergoeconomic factor* f_i will provide guidance in choosing the preferred strategy:

Table 5.11 Typical values for exergoeconomic factors

Equipment unit	f_i
Boilers	$\leq 50\,\%$
Heat exchangers	$\leq 55\,\%$
Compressors	$35\,\% \leq f_i \leq 75\,\%$
Pumps	$\geq 70\,\%$

- If f_i is high, it is advisable to investigate whether the cost overrun is reduced by simplifying the design to reduce investment, though somewhat undermining energy efficiency.
- If f_i is low, it is preferable to attempt to reduce cost increase through thermodynamic improvements, even with some increase in investment.

In any case, the effect of thermodynamic improvements must be investigated in equipment units of low exergetic efficiency, or with high values of exergy destruction or of the corresponding ratio. If any piece of equipment destroys exergy without contributing to lowering the investment or the costs of this or other equipment, its elimination should be considered. The subsystem with a higher relative cost overrun is the subsystem formed by the steam turbine + cascade condensation system (CCS), which would be the one for which improving actions should be considered, if optimizing the system.

References

1. Baasel WD (1976) Preliminary chemical engineering plant design. Elsevier Scientific Publishing Company, New York
2. Bandyopadhyay S (2001) Thermoeconomic optimization of combined cycle power plants. Energy Convers Manag 42:359–371
3. Besarati SM (2010) Multi-objective thermodynamic optimization of combined Brayton and inverse Brayton cycles using genetic algorithms. Energy Convers Manag 51:212–217
4. Frangopoulos C (1994) Application of the thermoeconomic functional approach to the CGAM problem. Energy 19(3):323–341
5. Marshall & Swift Equipment Cost Index (2012) M&S Index, available in Chemical Engineer. http://www.che.com. Accessed 2 May 2012
6. Spakovsky MR (1994) Application of engineering functional analysis to the analysis and optimization of the CGAM problem. Energy 19(3):343–364
7. Tsatoris G (1994) Exergoeconomic evolution and optimization of energy systems—application to the CGAM problem. Energy 19(3):287–321
8. Tsatsaronis G (1993) Thermoeconomic analysis and optimization of energy systems. Prog Energy Combust Sci 19(3):227–257

Appendix A
Use of MHBT for the Practical Case

The practical case has been solved using the MHBT application [1] which has been updated and improved. In this annex an explanation is given of how the MHBT has been used to solve the case.

As introduced in Chap. 1, an Aspen Plus® simulation (`Asp1001`) has been done obtaining the thermodynamic data (`WB1001`), and a flowsheet (`Doc1001`). To start with, a RPI classification analysis has been done (`Doc2003`) and afterwards the MHBT has been used. The information given in `WB1001`, `Doc1001` and `Doc2003` is an input for the MHBT software to obtain the exergy and thermoeconomic analyses.

When running the MHBT, as a first step the language, currency and initials to identify the SRE streams and the auxiliary streams and equipment must be chosen. The auxiliary equipment and streams are those used in Aspen Plus® to simulate complex equipment using the Aspen Plus® existing blocks (i.e. the most simple gas turbine simulation needs at least three Aspen Plus® Blocks: two compressors and a chemical reactor representing the air compressor, the combustion chamber and the expansion turbine).

Although in the new version of the MHBT software, the user is allowed to define the initials of each SRE stream, auxiliary streams and equipment, the first initial must be selected in each case as a letter at the end of the alphabet. This will ensure that the SRE streams in the workbook (`WB1001`) are located in the final columns of the spreadsheet. Afterwards, data from the thermodynamic and matter balances must be supplied to the workbook as they are obtained from the simulation (`WB1001`).

After completing the abovementioned steps, the user will be asked if any changes in the streams' direction must be done. In our case, no changes are needed as there are no auxiliary streams or pieces of equipment. The application will then calculate the incidence matrix, the matter, energy and exergy balances and the relative destruction of exergy.

E. Querol et al., *Practical Approach to Exergy and Thermoeconomic Analyses of Industrial Processes*, SpringerBriefs in Energy,
DOI: 10.1007/978-1-4471-4622-3, © The Author(s) 2013

Table A.1 Assigned exergetic costs vector

Unit	R	P	I
E914	−93103 + 93104	94107 − 94106	
E915	93104 − 93105	94105 − 94106	
E916	93105	94104 − 94105	93106
M922	95102 + 97109	94101	
E924[a]	94101 + 98102	94102	98103
P922	W04	−94102 + 94103	
E925	95101 − 95102	−94103 + 94104	
T971	94107 − 94108	W03	
E921	94108 − 94109	97108 − 97106	
S921	97108	95101 + 96101	
V921	96101	96102	
M921	94109 + 96102	97101	
E923	97101 − 97102	−97105 + 97106	
E922[b]	97102 + 98101 − 98102	97103	
P921	W05	97104 − 97103	
S922	97104	97105 + 97109	
P981[c]	98104 + W06	98101	

[a] The target of this piece of unit E924 is to destroy exergy as for technical reasons a condenser is needed to change from vapour to liquid the fluid phase before being pumped. This classification is unusual and is not the one used when analysing other types of exchangers

[b] As in E924, although in this case the exiting cooling fluid is not a loss, as it is used to cool down E924

[c] This classification is different from the one usually used in the case of pumps as the fluid entering the pump comes from outside of the control zone. Thermodynamically this pump increases the exergy of the fluid (as in the other cases) but from a thermoeconomic point of view this pump needs two different resources. These must be provided from outside the process to the pump, being: the entering fluid and the work needed to drive the pump. This way the classification of stream 98104 is the same regardless the aggregation level of the process that has been chosen

The RPI classification is the next step. In this case, the information in `Doc2003` is supplied by piece of equipment, as in Table A.1. MHBT uses this information to build the R, P, I matrices.

The information that the user has previously supplied allows the MHBT to calculate the exergy of resources, products and losses and the efficiency and the relative exergy destruction in the process.

For the exergetic cost calculation the following step is needed. As in Sect. 4.3, additional equations must be supplied considering the economics of the process. The MHBT application will ask the user for additional equations, going from the easiest to the most controversial ones:

1. Exergetic cost of losses. Each loss has an Eq. 4.15 associated. It is applied to streams 93106, 98103 so two additional equations are added.

2. Exergetic cost of resources entering the system. In this case a singularity appears: there are two different types of resources according to their stream's nature in this process: matter streams and work streams, and as such they must be treated in a different way.

   a. In the case of the matter streams, they come from outside of the process, so Eq. 4.14 should be applied to streams 93103 and 98104 adding two additional equations.
   b. In the case of the exergetic cost of work streams, it will be misleading to apply Eq. 4.14 as it will imply that these resources are obtained from a different process (power bought in the market). As this process has been designed to produce work, the net work produced by it must consider the work consumed by its pumps (self-consumption) which will be the main difference between the gross and net power generation of the process. Therefore power produced by T971 and power consumed by the pumps must have the same unit cost. Equation 4.22 is applied to give the same unit exergetic cost to the power produced and consumed by the process. This equation has been applied to all the work streams (considered as consumption) in the cycle. W01, W05, W06 adding three more equations.

3. Branchings. As the process in not producing any by-product, the rest of equations needed to square the cost matrix must be obtained using the R or P principles in those equipment units with more than one exiting stream that have not been previously considered (losses). The R-principle is used in E914, E915, E925, T971, E921, E923, E922 (between 98101 and 98102); whereas the P-principle has been applied in S921, S922, having nine equations more.

When all this information has been supplied the MHBT application is able to calculate the exergetic cost of all streams.

To determine the thermoeconomic cost, the following information is required by the MHBT:

- The fixed costs vector Z that contains the costs of every equipment unit in the process. In this example the information is in another `Workbook` and to be submitted to the MHBT. In this case the first cell form the additional workbook contains the Equipment Unit name and next to it there is a cell containing the fixed cost Z of the piece of equipment.
- The thermoeconomic cost of the resource streams entering the process, which in this case are streams 93103 (free of charge) and 98104.

After submitting these data, the MHBT application is able to complete the calculations. These calculations will give as result:

- The thermoeconomic cost of all the streams (including the thermoeconomic and unit exergoeconomic cost of resources and products and the thermoeconomic cost of losses).

- The exergy destruction in the system and per piece of equipment.
- The relative overcost of producing each stream.
- Three indexes: the loss coefficient, the significance factor and the loss component.

Reference

1. Querol E, Gonzalez-Regueral B, Perez-Benedito JL (2011) Novel application for exergy and thermoeconomic analysis of processes simulated with Aspen Plus®. Energy 36:964–974

MIX
Papier aus verantwortungsvollen Quellen
Paper from responsible sources
FSC® C105338

If you have any concerns about our products,
you can contact us on
ProductSafety@springernature.com

In case Publisher is established outside the EU,
the EU authorized representative is:
Springer Nature Customer Service Center GmbH
Europaplatz 3, 69115 Heidelberg, Germany

Printed by Libri Plureos GmbH
in Hamburg, Germany